MW01041911

Adventure
of

Becoming
an
AIRLINE PILOT

My Story as a High School Dropout
Who Succeeded by Doing What I Dreamed

George Flavell

Copyright © 2006 by George Flavell

ISBN 0-7414-3130-0

Published by:

INFINITY
PUBLISHING.COM

1094 New DeHaven Street, Suite 100
West Conshohocken, PA 19428-2713
Info@buybooksontheweb.com
www.buybooksontheweb.com
Toll-free (877) BUY BOOK
Local Phone (610) 941-9999
Fax (610) 941-9959

Printed in the United States of America

Printed on Recycled Paper

Published April 2006

NOTE:

This story is nonfiction. It is the story of a boy who failed high school, went into the service during the Korean War, learned to be a journeyman machinist while there, took flying lessons on the GI Bill, and made something of his life in aviation. All of the names are real people who were there as I remember them, in scenarios that I have recalled and depicted. The aircraft, the places, the conversations are all as real as I remember them. It is said that we remember the good things and forget the bad things. I must be very lucky; for all the things that I have written, I am pleased with every word, with every name and with every face that each acquaintance or friendship brings back. If I have written something that offends someone, it is not intended.

The Author

CONTENTS

i

PREFACE

Titling this book as an "Adventure" is accurate and meets all of Webster's definitions for that word. There was no reason to believe, in my wildest dreams, that the life I would live was even remotely possible. I have no college degree. I did not even have a high school diploma, after being the first senior to fail in twenty years. Described as a daydreamer without direction, I had little interest in school. I tried to join the Air Force before graduation, but failed. In November 1950, the Korean War was continuing. I was 18 now and received a telegram accepting me into the Air Force. Three years later, when I was overseas, I took and passed a GED test with high enough grades that my high school approved and gave me a diploma. Getting an education as an aircraft machinist in the service helped me later when being hired by United Airlines, and once again, I was close to aviation. I learned to fly on the GI Bill and went on to fly as a pilot with several airlines. Changing of airlines after furloughs, shutdowns, or my own decisions most often led me to make the move as a captain. Unbelievably, I did this six times between 1963-1992. The majority of experienced pilots will say, "Impossible." Tell them to read this book. You can also mention that I was a "MEC" (Master Executive Chairman) and a Director of ALPA (Air Line Pilots Association) until deregulation went into affect in 1978, and the world of the lifetime airline job disappeared. Many did not believe it then; all believe it now.

I have written this book as an encouragement to all who seek a flying career, as there are many opportunities still there. The route you take to get there varies tremendously. I have shared the cockpit with colonels, doctors, lawyers and others who did not remain in their first profession and who have chosen to become airline pilots. I once had a retired U.S.

Navy Admiral sent to accompany me from a hotel to the offices of an aircraft manufacturer. Since he knew I had been hired over the phone, he asked me how I knew Captain McCabe, Chief Pilot, and I replied, "He was my instructor on the DC-9-32CF about 11 years ago." He asked me what aircraft I had flown in the service. My answer was to tell him that the U.S. Air Force would not let an airman 2nd class fly their airplanes. He wondered aloud why I would be chosen to be a DC-10 Production Test Pilot. I ventured, "Because I am rated and experienced in that aircraft, with considerable international experience, and over 20,000 hours of large aircraft time." He said, "Welcome aboard."

I wrote this book for those who want to get into aviation and for those who dreamt of aviation and could not have it; for those who sacrificed their dreams to provide for others and could not afford it; and the others who lost their dreams after attaining it; and for reasons of physical examinations, performance standards, or personal problems, as well as many other obstacles to being in this business. Any of the above could well have been me except for the fact that I was very lucky and had the chance to live it.

Also, I wrote this book for my beautiful daughters, Denise and Leslie; for my son, George, the man I would like to have been like had I not been off flying, and for Stephen, whom we lost at 19 years old. This will suffice as a scrapbook of sorts of what their father was doing on all the holidays and distant employments when I could not be with them.

Thank you to my wonderful wife, Lane, who assisted in proofing the text, correcting and helping me with the "Word Program," and for chasing the cats off the computer, as well as giving me the solitude to take myself back to distant worlds and long-ago times.

This is not complete without mentioning my mother Josephine who flew in her youth. I placed her in the left seat of a Cessna 172SP on her 90th birthday. She flew well, from Sarasota to Boca Grande and back, holding her altitude.

OVERSEAS NATIONAL AIRWAYS

1974, Oakland to Honolulu

The Author

There are few pictures taken of me in uniform, much less while flying. This picture was a candid snapshot by Bill Whitesell, Flight Engineer, with a new camera that he had purchased. We were flying 254 passengers on a DC-8-63. How do I know how many passengers were onboard? We were a charter airline; we were always full. How I wish I could just turn away and actually be there again. ONA was the best airline I ever flew with, and hundreds of us still go to reunions, even though they left the airline business in 1978 while profitable. All retirement plans were over funded, and vacations and bonuses were paid.

CHAPTER 1

Early Interest

When I was young, my grandparents would take me to visit my Great Uncle Harry and Aunt Minnie. There was nothing for an eight-year-old to do at their house because of being constantly reminded that this or that thing could break. On one visit, I found a metal airplane; it was huge—the wings were longer than my arms, and it was so heavy I could hardly lift it. When I made my entrance into the living room, Aunt Minnie shouted, "Oh dear, be careful with that; it is really a doorstop." It was a Tri-Motor Ford design with corrugated skin but made of cast iron, which would have put a hole in the floor before breaking any part of it. Thereafter on subsequent visits, they would reluctantly get this "toy" out for me, and I would spend the entire time on the floor taxiing it around on its free turning main landing gear wheels and caster tail wheel.

My next aircraft was a balsa wood model that was even larger and much lighter and hung from the ceiling above my bed. A family friend had constructed it for me, a Douglas DC-4, four engine aircraft; it was much too fine and detailed to be allowed to use as a toy. I used to stand on my bed where I could reach up to twist a few turns in the string. This allowed me to watch it as it slowly unwound. One day I decided to be a little more bold, as pilots are wont to be and made a few extra turns in the string and created a really neat spin; unfortunately, the string broke, and the right wing caught me behind the knee and I collapsed on it. Despite the crash scene, I would walk away, but the model aircraft was a "total loss." My explanation to the "authorities" was accepted about the same way the FAA would have dealt with it being "grounded." When I was older, I bought an expensive wooden propeller designed for a real gas engine model airplane and rigged it up on the handlebars of my bike where I could look through the wind-driven prop. I added a handlebar thumb bell, modified to sound like bullets thudding into enemy aircraft; it may have helped win World War II. Next, I had a balsa wood glider, weighted at the nose so that it could be whirled by hand, yet it had movable elevators at the tail, allowing control of climb, dive and flare for landing. The process of whirling it also created dizziness; a feature that this balsa wood glider pilot would succumb to causing occasional crashes. A slightly similar instrument flying problem exists in the real world, such advanced simulation for such a reasonable price. The bloody knees or palms that occurred with my crashes were not a simulation, however.

CHAPTER 2

Stepping Stones

The Korean War began in June 1950, just as I did *not* graduate from high school—the first "senior" to fail in 20 years. I did not feel like going to summer school, which was nothing new; I was sick of school. I tried to enlist in the Air Force, but they did not want me because I was missing a toe from a farm tractor accident. I tried the Marine Corps and the Army Paratroopers; all turned me down, same reason. I applied to the phone company to become a lineman, but they said I could not climb poles with a missing toe. I took a job with a tool & die company; I did not tell them about the toe.

In November, my mother intercepted three telegrams, one from each of the branches of services that had turned me down. She only showed me the one from the Air Force, which said they would accept me as soon as I was 18. On November 10, 1950, a few weeks after my 18th birthday, I was sworn into the U.S. Air Force. This happened with a large group of others on a North Philadelphia train platform, awaiting departure to Lackland AFB, Texas. I would now be as close to flying, as I might ever be. It was a fortunate choice, and I elected to be an aviation machinist for the same reason.

After nine months of training at Chanute AFB, Illinois, my squadron was ready for orders to get out of there. It had taken two months before getting into school, and every day during that time we had to fall out at 0700, the same time as the squadrons going to school. The only difference after roll call as we stood at ease was the school squadrons marching off to school, whereas the others were getting duty assignments. This consisted of washing pots and pans at the mess hall, firing coal furnaces, sweeping streets, etc. It came to our notice that the squadrons graduating ahead us, who had not yet received orders to ship out, were also included in these same duties. We planned to prevent that from happening to us. When we graduated, we picked a leader to march us away until out of sight, and then we went to the PX area for bowling, movies, and cheeseburgers. Before the duty sergeant figured out what had happened to the missing squadron, our departure orders came through.

We were going to California and then overseas; we were ready. After a short staging delay of three days at a base near the Sacramento River, our now larger group was ready for orders to move out. When they finally came, they transported us on a ferryboat in the Sacramento River that would take us to the San Francisco Embarcadero. We planned what we would do once in the city but instead we docked next to a large troop ship, the "Edwin D. Patrick" and up the gangway we went, destination Yokohama, Japan. Goodbye, San Francisco, maybe someday.

After going below, decks and selecting from bunks that were arranged four high, I wisely chose the top bunk, avoiding a rain of vomit that I suspected might occur. Several of us returned topside to see the city and the Golden Gate Bridge; something all of us hoped to see again. As we sailed underneath the bridge, this last recognizable vestige of the USA, the ship's engines made a noticeable speed increase. The slightly cooler air and sight of vast openness lent itself to a feeling of great adventure in crossing the Pacific Ocean.

A bullhorn voice boomed, "Now hear this, now hear this, all military personnel report below deck to your assigned compartments." Pausing to read the deck diagram's placard, painted on a bulkhead, I noticed I was going down below the waterline. How nice, I thought, I could have been a submariner, if I liked that sort of thing.

In our compartments, another PA address with a less windy bass advised that a watertight door drill would be accomplished and all personnel was warned to stay away from the emergency doors in these compartments. For those who had not paid much attention before, they did now, and realized what that rack and pinion drive was for on those big steel doors. The doors were remotely controlled, in case of hull damage, and sealed the compartments off from the rest of the ship. This meant that any personnel still alive would likely drown. My second plan was to go out the hole that let the water in, if possible. My first plan was not to be inside the compartment when the door closed. A few of the troops voiced claustrophobic feelings as the door sealed both our access and airflow. A tomb-like silence existed except for the now muffled perpetual heartbeat of the engines. Looking at the faces of the others, I think everyone had my first plan in mind for the future.

When the emergency drill ended and the doors ground their way open, a noticeable release of tension filled the compartment. I sensed the ship as being in deeper water, the pitch stretched out as well as a slower rolling motion, a steady boring rhythm. Fresh sea air again flowed into our compartment. It was not long before I caught the sudden foul smell of seasickness. It usually starts with one, and then spreads quickly until almost all are affected. The noise and smell of those who thought they might prefer dying got worse. Some who had the presence to be considerate gathered around garbage cans, placed for just that purpose. All compartments on our deck were affected.

Those of us who did not get seasick were selected for garbage can duty, hauling the vomit to the upper deck, going back to the fantail, and dumping it overboard. I remember thinking at the time, if I am in the air force, why am I traveling on a ship? I wondered if all the navy swabbies fly. Up on deck, we could see the setting sun illuminating the Farallon Islands in our distant wake. The sun finally disappeared, and the air became cold. I went below to climb via the edge of the lower bunks to my penthouse bunk, all the while avoiding arms and legs belonging to the bodies in the lower bunks, those who no longer cared if they were stepped on or not.

After the next call to haul the cans topside, we learned this was pretty good duty because those of us well enough to work were allowed at any hour to enjoy the ship's mess where the active crew ate. The biggest discomfort was sleeping where the smell was strong and the occasional groan and gagging broke through the sound of the ship's screws turning. Some on the lower bunks I noticed were sleeping with their raincoats on.

The next day was clear and cool, and all military personnel were ordered topside while the work details would get busy hosing things down in the compartments. The three of us again with other compartment teams were put to use watching airmen lying on the decks, making sure no one was about to roll off, some likely not caring if they did. We walked around with a carton of ice cream sandwiches, enjoying the fresh air, while the poor slobs who were sick lay on the deck looking worse when they saw us. We had no mercy; after all, we had to live with their defects.

A few days later, almost all were back to normal, and we three lost our rights to the ship's mess and had to eat with the rest. Going topside and watching the ship plow through the waves, I wished that I could visit the bridge and see how they navigated and wondered if they had an auto pilot or were hand steering, etc. I sort of enjoyed this life and wondered if I had made a mistake in not joining the navy. It was probably closer to reality to dream of being a captain of a boat than to being an airline pilot, but since these are only dreams, why not dream big.

On the tenth day, standing on the fantail and watching our wake, I suddenly became aware of birds. We had lost the birds on the third day, but now they were back—a sure sign we were getting closer to land. These were slightly different than the ones we had seen leaving California. There were also flying fish skipping the surface and crashing into a wave or back into the sea. On the next morning, everyone was advised to be topside if wanting to see the first sight of Japan. It was not long before someone noticed something in the distance and pointed to it. I looked, but it looked like a cloud on the horizon, yet everyone was still watching. Then I saw it and exclaimed, "That cloud is snow on Mt. Fujiyama." A soldier, somewhat older than I standing close by, corrected me, "You can say Fujiyama or you can say Mount Fuji, but since yama means mountain, you would be saying Mount Fuji Mountain." By now, Fujiyama was in all its glory, a beautiful sight rising out of the sea. Funny to be thinking that only five years before we expected to lose about a million men to conquer Japan. My dad was a marine.

In Yokohama, we lived in tents for 30 days. During that time, we all ran out of money. We ate at the military mess hall, but not having any money for anything else was really getting everyone edgy. I had talked to the payroll officer who told me he could not help because all our pay records were in transit and not available. Several days of lying around in this twelve-man tent finally got to me. I rolled out of my sack, a lower one now for convenience, and said, "I'm going to the chaplain." A voice from the other end of the tent mimicked what I said followed by "poor baby." I ignored the sarcasm and said, "Yeah, this poor baby needs a beer and some cigarettes as well as a change of scenery down at the PX, watching you guys play poker for toothpicks is making me sick. I'm going to complain for all of us since we haven't been paid for 60 days."

"You do all your crying for yourself, baby; we don't need your whining to help us," said the only voice that responded.

At the chaplain's office, he waved me to a chair. I explained the situation, using the lack of razor blades, toothpaste and deodorant as the reasons for an advance of pay since that seemed more appropriate, considering his upward chain of command. He asked if I was the only one, and I mentioned the rest are probably in the same situation. He reached for the phone, called the base finance officer, and told him to prepare an advance payroll for the men who came off the ship from Chanute AFB. The phone barked loudly with the reply that he had already talked to one of us and had explained why it was impossible. The chaplain softly spoke in the phone, "It is an advance, Major. Make the advance and do it now, as I am sending one of those men over immediately." I did not hear the reply because the voice on the phone was not loud now.

Back in the barracks, I laid down on my bunk without looking at anyone. I waited until someone spoke up, asking if the chaplain had patted my head. "Naw, he didn't do anything like that," I said, "he just had the major over in finance advance me $100," which I held up. "Hey, what kind of money is that anyhow?" said one. I explained that this is "Script," and it is the military money used throughout the Pacific. I fanned out 10 tens, the highest denomination possible. "Well, did you tell him about the rest of us?" said one. "Yeah I did, told him you were all fine without any help just like "yawl" said."

"You better be kidding," a voice said, as they all started out of the tent. "Wait a minute," I shouted and they paused. "Just remember no whining or crying, and I think the one that called me 'Baby' should kiss my baby ass."

"We will see that he does that after we get our money." I left the tent to go to the PX to avoid them, just in case they were serious.

In the end, we gradually split up, going to different assignments. Some went to Korea; some stayed in Japan; a couple went to Guam; the others and I went to Clark AFB, Philippine Islands, where the 13th Air Force was based. I was assigned to the 24th Aircraft Repair Squadron. At least we flew there on a C-54, the same as a DC-4, like the model that I had fallen on. Once at Clark Field, we were hustled off in our dress blue winter uniforms to an open-air chapel where we sweated in the tropical heat. The chaplain proceeded to warn us of the distinct danger for our souls in this area of the world. "In particular," said the chaplain, "Angeles City, just a few kilometers outside the gate with 135 bars and hordes of young women only interested in taking your money." The sweating and the interest in the sermon improved noticeably for just those few moments, but an officer mentioned our warm clothing to the chaplain and suggested all could get more information at the next Sunday service. One more speaker had to warn us about the cobra snake. "If you are bitten, you have a 50/50 chance of dying, after which the odds would go downhill if you did not get an anti-venom shot or raised your heartbeat by running." Umm, I think most of us vowed to die in town first.

As for "Angeles City," it was like a Wild West setting, dirt streets that turned to mud during the rainy season and horse-drawn carriages. The people were friendly, honest and poor. The barrios behind the main street were off limits at all times to military personnel, and the main street was off limits between 2200 hours and 0700 hours. In other words, no military people were in town overnight; well, not quite, they could be safely back in the barrios with a friend. One could also be out of sight if staying in quarters on the street, but not quite safe since the military "Air Police" could raid these buildings.

The penalty for being caught was one stripe, which also equates to one pay grade lower. I remember seeing a former master sergeant (six stripes) wearing a shirt without any stripes. I did not know the man, but I could tell by the different shirt coloration where the rank had been. He seemed happy. I wondered at the time how they would penalize anyone after all the stripes were gone; just maybe you could live in town…naw, but then I only had one stripe to lose. One night I decided to stay in town. It was one of the few two-story buildings in town. I was in the upstairs forward bedroom at about 0300 when a roaring sound of 6x6 trucks came into town in a massive air police raid. The screaming ladies and swearing GIs could be heard blocks away. I grabbed my clothes, shoes and hat, stuffed them in a pillowcase, and with just skivvies on, jumped out on the forward tin roof over the street in full view. Anyone seeing me probably thought I was going to jump to the ground, to be eventually caught. However, I turned and climbed onto the sloping tin roof that covered the top of the house, inching upward and rearward, creating some noise that caused me to pause after each advance. Away from the street now, I suddenly noticed a naked GI silhouetted by the moon, squatting like a gargoyle on the peak of the roof. I suggested he move below the roofline to avoid being seen. The gargoyle replied, "Mind your f------ business." I thought that was very appropriate and very funny at the same time. I barely contained my laughter. I rolled slowly onto my back, causing a little more noise from the roof and hissing whispers from the rooftop.

A little later, a girl from the house appeared and whispered to me, "Do you want company?" I replied, "Why not." Thinking, if I am caught, I do not want anyone to think I am related to the gargoyle. He was hissing away and complaining about the oil can noise of the roof as she came crawling toward me. The noises in the street were growing louder so we knew that the heavy hand of the law was getting closer. The girl was near and finally snuggled close to me. She asked me my name, I told her and she replied, "I am Pilar." Lying still, on our backs, looking at the stars, I started to get a laughing jag. This irritated the gargoyle, and the anger in his whispered threats only added to this idiotic situation. I had received a letter recently from my mother asking me to tell her more of what I am doing. Putting that thought into the present picture almost sent me off the roof. Some trucks were rolling by with large loads of GIs standing and yelling in the back. Others were stopping close to where we were. We could hear the APs coming up the steps to the second floor, and with great effort, I controlled my humor. I thought surely we were caught, but the scene changed somewhat quickly as though a fast and noisy summer storm was not there anymore. When I looked up over my shoulder, the gargoyle was gone. My single stripe was safe.

The fights in town were another recreational treat. The ones in the bar were usually knife fights or bottle fights; plain fistfights were always ordered to go outside. The reason for this I suppose was that no one wanted to interfere with the knives or the bottles. The knives were flip knifes, a hollow split bone handle that concealed the entire knife blade until the handle was unlatched and both ends flipped around 180 degrees, leaving the blade fully extended. A long knife results from this. A knife fight could be watched at reasonably close quarters because the combatants needed to watch each other.

Usually the fight is about money, a woman, or honor and accompanied by alcohol, swearing and threats of death. Much sweating and little movement goes on until someone speaks up and says, "Shame, one's going to die and the other gets life." The combatants usually leave as good friends, and the action is over. The bottle fights are more active and need more room, so if they are close to your table it is best to move. The fistfights being outside were most interesting during the rainy season, as long as you had a view from inside a building. The flying mud is a mess for close spectators. I had a friend riding in a horse-drawn Kalisa, during the rainy season, lean out to yell at me, forgetting about the mud spinning off the wheel. His complexion changed instantly.

On base, in the open-air barracks where 40 men live in each of four large rooms, there will be a fistfight about one or two times a month. This is pure enjoyment, much as the TV is at home. On base, there is no gambling allowed, but on payday some form of it slips by. Once I overheard our commanding officer complaining to the first sergeant that we had too many wimps in our outfit because they were playing

Monopoly of all things and getting into serious fights about it. The first sergeant had to explain that they were playing for real money. The CO sounded impressed and satisfied by this explanation.

Really sophisticated gambling took place in Manila, the capital of the Philippines. Ernie Bell, my friend who waved from the Kalisa and got mud in his face, was the all-round expert on the history of the islands. His minor course must have been gambling odds because he kept the two of us in booze. We would play roulette, him playing red, and me playing black. What I would lose he would win and vis-à-vis. In the meantime, we were served complimentary drinks. When green would come up, we both would lose, but it did not appear often enough to make the drinks costly.

After our first year, we were eligible for rest & recreation, and we boarded a Navy Attack Transport Ship, the USS Pickaway to proceed to Hong Kong. Some fun, we sailed through a typhoon in the China Sea. Rumor had it that the lifeboats had torn loose on deck, but after we survived, I did not see any evidence of that. The biggest problem is the flying vomit again and the additional time at sea that I was accumulating. This would make four days roundtrip, so I will have 15 days total upon return to Manila. Hong Kong is an island with a built-up business area and many things to see. Kowloon is across the river and is an area of hotels and residential sections. The transportation back and forth was by boat and cost only four cents per person. I bought a chess set and a beautiful nude ivory statue, the rest I spent on serious Chinese food and drink.

The 24th Aircraft Repair Squadron Hangar is where we did depot overhaul on Douglas C-47s or DC-3s, as known in civilian use. Depot overhaul is the military term for effectively returning the entire aircraft to as new a condition as possible. I knew the nomenclature of every major part on those C-47s. I had a friend who was an airborne radio operator in another squadron who had to check out the HF radios installed on these aircraft before returning to service. A lot of his work was on the weekends, and I was free to climb aboard the aircraft and sit in the cockpit. I envied his ability to power up the electrical system onboard and talk to stations around the world on high frequency radio. Sitting in the cockpit, other instrumentation would come to life as a byproduct of powering the electrical system, letting me appreciate the complexity of the aircraft. Sitting in the captain's seat allowed me to dream dreams and admire the pilots who could fly them. At least it was the real thing, all those switches, how complicated it must be, how far beyond my education and realistic ability to achieve.

At the end of this assignment, I rotated back to the USA. Of course, it would be by boat. It took 21 days to San Francisco so I wound up with 36 days at sea, more time at sea than many real sailors. My new orders read "Assigned to the 95th Field Bomb Wing" at Biggs AFB, El Paso, Texas. This was a SAC (Strategic Air Command) Base where they had B-36 bombers, a very secret jet bomber in that day. It exemplified the cusp of change going on between airframe builders and available engines to power them. It required six Pratt &

Whitney, 28-cylinder engines mounted as pushers and four Jet Engines, two on each outboard wing. This ten-engine aircraft used combinations of the old and new technologies. A handful of six throttles and four thrust levers as they were called on the jet's engines. The large radial engines were the biggest ever mass-produced and the end of the piston engine use in very heavy aircraft. At the same time, Jet Engine development was picking up the needed thrust to obsolete them.

My enlistment was complete with an early-out offer as the air force budget had been slashed, with the Korean Armistice, allowing those who had less than a year to serve to take an early discharge.

Back home, in Pennsylvania, I found that many things had changed, including me. I was impressed with what I had seen of California and thought a great deal about moving there. I was working as a machinist, but still thinking about flying. My personal life was complicated by a brief marriage to a lovely girl who would never be able to leave her family. It was something I did not see soon enough, and we did not last.

One day while reading the employment section of a Philadelphia newspaper, I noticed an advertisement for a machinist position at United Airlines. It required moving and living in San Francisco. Wow, tough choice if that one does not have my name on it, nothing ever will. I had to apply at a state unemployment office in North Philadelphia where a United Airlines personnel man would be interviewing. I took some written tests and later sat with two older and probably more experienced people. Being the last interviewed during a long wait worried me. Surely, they had greater experience and better qualifications. As each one left, they looked pleased. When I went in, the interviewer came to his feet, greeted me by name, and asked me to take a seat by his desk, mentioning some paperwork he had to finish. I presumed the paperwork to be important for the previous applicants.

Without knowing if any vacancies existed, I continued to worry. He abruptly asked me what I had in the bag. I had carried a shaving kit filled with a handful of tools that I had made while in training with the Air Force. With sudden interest, he asked if he could look at them, and he emptied them gently on his desk. He studied each one in turn and then picked the most complex, the tapered Helical Reamer, and asked me to describe the steps I used to make it. I replied that I blanked out the profile including the taper on a lathe, did the reamer flutes and end square on a milling machine, then did the heat treating necessary and the grinding of the flutes. "Really?" he said. He turned and retrieved my application and asked me what I had chiefly worked on when I was in the air force and I replied aircraft only. The next question, "If I hire you, when can you leave?" I said, "Tomorrow," and he turned and wrote out a positive space complimentary ticket on a United Airlines flight to San Francisco, leaving in three days.

As I was checking into the Ben Franklin Hotel in San Mateo, California, I noticed a UAL flight crew in the lobby checking in. It included the crew that had brought me from Philadelphia. One of those flight attendants came over to me and said, "I see you found the hotel okay," and at the same time, the pilot came over and she introduced me as a new hire at the SFO, Mainliner Overhaul Base and that I had been on their flight. He shook my hand and cheerfully wished me well and introduced me to the rest of his cockpit crew. The captain going out of his way to do that really pleased me. I was still dealing with military protocol, where pilots are all officers, and where I would not have been so warmly received. I wanted to fly so much. If only I could have been hired as cabin crew, I probably would have never done anything else.

I suspected that my hiring was decided on my USAF machinist experience in an aircraft overhaul base. I also knew that United Airlines was flying the DC-7s with their turbo-compound engines at altitudes well above twenty thousand feet and setting new transcontinental speed records every so often. They were also having a number of engine failures using high blower operation for power. As it turned out, the UAL engine overhaul section was very busy because of this situation. I gained a lot of knowledge of the powerful "Wright 3350 power plants" that coincidently produced 3350 horsepower. My main job was to grind "Silver Plated" knuckle (articulating) rod pins to within $1/10^{th}$ of a thousandth of an inch without any taper. This was done using a precision grinding machine, which was left running twenty-four hours a day, keeping all moving parts and fluids warm. We had about 50 different sizes, so that an error on a larger dimension could be re-ground to correct the error to a needed smaller size. This option lasts only as long as it takes to be down to the smallest size, when they would have to be re-plated. I also worked on the cooling caps for the exhaust gas turbine section. Each section recovers 150 horsepower with three installed on each engine, an 1800 horsepower recovery.

Living in San Mateo, California, was a pleasure in 1955. I lived in a large antebellum-type boarding house just off the Highway 101 Freeway. There were perhaps six rooms used for boarders and only men. The elderly owner was a barber, and his wife ran the house, much like the military: make your own beds and leave the door open when not in your bedroom. She would pack a lunch for you and/or provide meals for an extra charge. I took only the lunch.

A United Airlines First Officer, Courtney Bennett was one of the boarders and so we had a little in common but did not socialize. One day, Courtney asked me if I would like to go for a ride over to Hayward Airport, on the other side of the San Francisco Bay. I said, "Sure," and we went out to his "Canary Yellow Lincoln Convertible." I was thinking, wow, what a lifestyle. On the way, he mentioned that he had bought a PT-19 and that if I was interested I could go along on a short test flight. Sure, I am ready. The flight was short, a couple of steep turns and a loop that really made my day. What a guy, what a life—I guess you have to be born to that. Courtney said he had to do about an hour's work on the aircraft and told me there was a coffee shop inside the terminal. I started to decline to see if he needed help, but at that instant, my eye caught a sign that said *Learn to Fly*. During that day, at that moment, my life was on the edge of a dramatic change.

CHAPTER THREE

Learning to Fly

Fairchild Air Services was located at Hayward, California, and was owned by a former Trans World Airline Captain named Ken Fairchild. When I first went into the airport building, I noticed three flight schools and a restaurant, but only the restaurant seemed to be interested in walk-in business. The other two, Tower Aviation and Lustig Air Services, had signs that said *Flying – Back Shortly*.

At Fairchild, there had been two young fellows talking flying, and I presumed them to be students from the conversations. I walked over to them. I asked how much flying lessons cost. One reached under the counter and handed me a brochure. We conversed for a time, while the man in the office looked up now and then. One of the students, whose status I now knew as accurate, spoke up and said that it would be a lot cheaper if I had the GI Bill. I replied that I did have it. The man in the office shot straight up, came around the counter, extending his hand and said, "I'm Ken Fairchild; if you have the GI Bill, you are going to learn to fly, and I am going to teach you. Just one question," he asked, "Do you like hamburgers?" As I hesitated, he said, "It's important." "Yes," I replied. "Good, then there's nothing else to worry about then, because in this business, son, you are going to eat many hamburgers." Funny question, but in the early months and years, and I guess to this day, I sometimes think about that question and wonder if I didn't like hamburgers would I have not been able to have a flying career? Naw, I like hot dogs, too.

Ken began teaching the first minute I showed up for a lesson. "Don't wear those sneakers next time; you need your heels to slide a little on the floor near the rudder pedals and wear a watch. Even if the aircraft has a clock, wear a watch. Pre-flighting the aircraft begins as soon as you lay eyes on it, much like your car if you parked in an unsafe parking lot. With an airplane, it is every time. Look at how it sits, does it look normal, is there anyone around it, is it being fueled, does anything look out of place, then do the close-up walk-around, starting at a particular place and ending back there. This is true even with the biggest aircraft. The student does everything a proficient pilot would do in the same sequence, but while you are in training, I will expect you, in subsequent lessons, to explain to me what you are looking at and what you are looking for. Pilots all over the world are doing what you will be doing today, as we speak, so this will go on for the rest of your flying career. Different answers are appropriate for the aircraft, engines, and airlines. Later on, when an examiner is following you around, he will ask you to expound even further to describe why something is there, how the failure of it would affect the aircraft, and/or the pilot, and whether you could safely go without it. At the point you can't think of anything else, move on to the next item quickly; if he has a question, he will ask it. The point being do not linger like there is more to explain, take charge before he starts thinking of questions he would like to know and move on."

One day after several ground and flight lessons, Ken asked me if I would like to go along on a multi-engine rating ride to observe. "Absolutely," I responded; he told me to meet him at the hangar, and I proceeded to go there. The twin-engine aircraft, a Cessna UC-78 or "Bamboo Bomber" as it was generally known because it not only had fabric wing coverings but it also had a fabric fuselage. As I was walking toward the aircraft, I noticed a Mason jar of water sitting near the tail of the aircraft although on the far side. The Bomber was not something I could fly, but I made the best of the walk-around that I could and stopped to inspect the Mason jar. It looked like water, but lifting it to my nose, I realized that it was white gas. It was sitting where the prop wash might blow it over, so I moved it further away and to one side, knowing that one of the mechanics must have it there for a reason.

The pilot and Ken who would administer a rating ride (additional notation on a pilot's license) had arrived and were waiting to board. I climbed onboard At Ken's command, we taxied out and took off, and after completing a number of required maneuvers and engine failures (simulated), we started a return to the airport. The pilot had lit a cigarette and somehow had dropped it in an area that allowed it to go through the floor and lay burning on a fabric coated with a nitrate dope. Ken took over the controls and raced to the runway that was now in view. Once on the ground, he taxied quickly to the hangar area, shut down, and ran out of the aircraft, shouting he saw some water. I raced after him and only caught him as he approached the aircraft while I braced myself and prevented him from getting his footing as he swore at me and shouted. The fumes from the jar suddenly alerted him, and he ran back to the hangar and got a water fire extinguisher from the hangar wall. Soon after, the soggy cigarette was removed; Ken lectured the pilot for smoking in that aircraft, but passed him otherwise, then turned to me and asked how I knew what was in the jar. I told him I had done a walk-around, and he smiled, then explained that the two of them had done a walk-around earlier, but that jar was not there then. "Good thing I taught you so good, kid."

California Airways took over. A couple of days later, I learned that Ken had sold the flight school to a couple of people who had vast experience in training military pilots at civilian airports during WW-II. They were Phil McManamy and Art Stagg. With their guidance, I was ready to solo, but for a week, the wind was too strong for any solo students and when it did calm down, they were both busy and delegated my solo to a pilot by the name of Dell Owens. We went out, and he said he needed a couple of takeoffs and landings and then proceeded to do a running takeoff from a 90-degree position, applying lots of power during this accelerating turn which really impressed me. Then he did a couple of touch and go landings, and then taxied back to runway 22 to allow me to demonstrate a couple of takeoffs and landings before he would solo me. At the conclusion of these, we went back to the beginning of the same runway for another takeoff that would be my first solo flight; heck, I was cool, I was ready. He mentioned that he would walk down the runway along the grass next to the dirt runway side of the paved runway. He would wave me on for three touch and go landings if they looked all right each time, otherwise I was to stop and pick him up. I stopped the aircraft 90 degrees to the runway as he had. He walked down the runway some distance, then waved me off. I sought to make the same kind of running takeoff he had done, but overdid the rate of turn and straightened out of the turn, heading directly for him. I kicked the left rudder and corrected this adventure before going very far. However, the last glimpse I had of him was the back of his head as he ran off the edge of the runway. I worried if he was going to wave me on for a touch and go or stop me when I landed. I tried my best to make it a safe looking approach and landing, but on short final, I could not see him anywhere. Then I saw him way over on the side, waving me on, so I touched gently, slowed to a fast taxi, and then concentrated on a smooth straight out departure. Finally, on the last landing, I saw that he was on the runway edge again, and I stopped as close as I could to pick him up. He jumped in, grinned, and said, "All's well that ends well."

After soloing, my training moved faster since I would be making progress combining dual instruction with solo practice. On my first, short, cross country, I was returning to Hayward and was in the Livermore Valley under an overcast that didn't look too thick but had a few small holes in it. I continued all the way to the Danville area and paralleled the

21

Hayward hills on the east side, all the while looking for a hole. I was sure that Hayward was in the clear, and all I had to do was get over the ridge. Doing so, I noticed a little sunshine back near the Livermore Airport. I decided to fly back that way. Suddenly, there was a big hole. After starting to climb, I realized that the hole was either smaller or I had misjudged. Turning tightly now, I continued to climb. I was gaining altitude, but not as fast as I would have straight ahead. I was finally on top. I was safe for now, but my world had changed; there was no land. I am on top of an endless sea of clouds, except for Mt. Diablo rising a couple of thousand feet above the clouds. The situation is beautiful but deadly. It does not matter that I have no instruments for I have no training and no way to navigate except the magnetic compass. If I fly higher or go further, I surely would find a hole, but fuel is a consideration too. The prognosis for my survival is poor.

I had expected to see the bay area and Hayward the way I had left it earlier in the day. Instead, I decided to fly toward the only view of earth I had—the mountain. As I progressed, I thought that perhaps close to the mountain, very close, there might be some ground visible at the lower altitudes. I could pull the power off and dive down the slope with visual reference. I had to be sure that I was diving toward the Livermore Valley though because in other directions there were high hills that would box me in. Using the compass, I turned north to fly past the point where I would turn south and approach this solution. I had to do this immediately for reasons of sunset and dwindling fuel. Something caught my eye. I saw a tiny speck; it could be a bird or another light airplane just further away. I turned toward the speck; if it was a bird, it had to be close, but it showed no movement in my turn; it had to be a plane. I continued, and soon I saw it was a light plane. It could be in trouble too, or it could be near an airport. In a few minutes, I noticed some patches of ground, and then in the distance an airport. I was already in position to start down but thought I would play it safe regarding fuel and gliding distance if I should run out. I was almost 4000 feet over the airport before I retarded the throttle, knowing now that even if I ran out of fuel I could glide it in anyway, I thought, those gages probably read lower than they really are. I entered the landing pattern a little high and left the power off to get down. I had been too cautious, and now I was diving to make the runway. I wanted to slip the aircraft as I had seen my instructors do, but I did not have the experience to do that. I just did not want to go around. I made a fast wheel landing, held it on the ground, while using brakes to slow it for the fast arriving end of the runway, and just made it. Taxiing into the ramp area, I saw a man signaling me into a parking spot. As I set the brakes, I also reached for the magneto switches to kill the engine, but before I could reach them, the engine died.

The man came to my door that was open now and asked me if I wanted fuel. I nodded yes. I could not talk properly; it was then that I noticed my legs were shaking. When the fuel truck arrived, the driver came over and said, "Fill both tanks?" I nodded again...damn if I was not cool, if only my legs would quit shaking. About that time, the bullhorn in the fueling area asked if that was N1904V, and if it was to send the pilot into the office. Oh well, I knew I was overdue but concerned about my legs and voice. I did not know the name of the airport either, so I had to keep an eye out for that. It would be easy to become a legend. ("Kid came in here, out of fuel, couldn't talk, couldn't walk, and didn't know where he was.") I took the phone to talk to Art and explained that I had detoured a little...for weather. "Damn good judgment, son, we have had some real "hamburgers" that have tried to go up through a hole or something rather than detour. I wish all our students were like you; anyhow, sit tight, we are sending another pilot to pick you up since the weather is a little tight here." I was not too happy about having another pilot pick me up. I was alive at least, but just the same, I could have made it back. Just at that moment, the refueler came in the door and shouted in my direction and everyone else's, "What kind of fuel tanks do you have in that plane? I have never put that much in a Cessna 120 before." I said, "Yeah that's right, just a little bigger, enough for an extra hour." I then asked the man behind the desk for a business card; since they gave me such good service; I wanted to tell others. Buchanan Airport, Concord, California. Heck, I could fly home from here myself.

California Airways had been good for me. Phil and Art were both good and demanding of high standards, and I progressed quickly with the GI Bill behind me. I had a Private Pilot License in 30 days, a Commercial License in six months, and one month after that, I was a rated Flight Instructor and hired by the school.

Life was good; receiving pay to fly instead of paying to fly was better, but I was now working two jobs: United Airlines at night and flight instructing during the day. When I had a few hundred hours, I applied to United for a Second Officer position (Flight Engineer). A human resources man looked up my record with the company and said, "I'm afraid that you do not have the qualifications, son." He wouldn't elaborate but after pleading with him about things I am doing, he finally said, "You have been late six times in the last three months, and that is something that would get you fired the second time it happened if you were in the flight department." I explained that my flying job was extending into my duties in the machine shop, but that I always showed up only minutes late and always completed my shift assignments. I explained the priority of my flying was prime to me and that giving me a chance that would never happen in that position. He replied, "I'm sorry. I really think you should concentrate on the job you have." I could not fault him, but I knew he was not a pilot.

A couple of days later, I was late again, and the big boss and two supervisors called me into the office. They were good people doing their jobs. The big boss said, "Son, you have been late too much. I think you should sit down here and tell us what the problem is and maybe we can help." I said, "Well my problem is my flying job, and like the airlines, I cannot always work it out to exactly the few minutes involved." "Well son, you can see that you have to sit down and figure out what is more important—your flying or this here job." "I don't have to sit down to tell you the answer to that, sir...my flying is what I am going to do in this life." I expected to be fired, but they just looked at each other and one said, "OK George, go ahead, grind us some knuckle pins."

During the next few weeks, I did sort through my priorities and quit United Airlines. I compensated for the loss of income by giving up my boarding house room in San Mateo and moved into the parachute loft above the California Airways hangar at Phil's suggestion. The price was right. I bought a sleeping bag and pillow. Hamburgers were cheap, and maybe Ken Fairchild was right after all. During the next year, I flew maximum hours. Now I was thinking "Airlines" but as a "First Officer" (Copilot) with a smaller airline than United Airlines. I needed an Instrument Rating, and my GI Bill had run out. California Airways had been good, but they did not have any aircraft equipped for that. I had an offer from a school across the bay in San Carlos, Harper Aviation, and a modern, bigger operation. I made the change.

I was now flying Piper Tri-pacers, a very good training aircraft with the bungee cord coordination bundle loosened, so that pilot inputs could be better analyzed. I was now making more money and had access to better-equipped aircraft, making my way to the Instrument Rating possible. I found a great instructor, a United Airlines pilot, Bob Collins, a great young man who went on to become a Vice-President with United, although that didn't impress as much as his giving up a great flying job. Upon passing my written, oral and flight test for the instrument rating, I promptly went to a book that provided addresses for all major airlines worldwide, then started sending resumes to all that I would like. Strangely, as bold as that sounds, almost all of those letters were answered or jobs were offered over a period of about ten years. They must assume that one's qualifications are improving with time. In my most immediate situation, I got a call from California Airways, which still kept me in their good graces, telling me that they received a telegram for me from Aloha Airlines in Honolulu, offering me employment as a DC-3 copilot and if interested to call collect ASAP.

MUNICIPAL AIRPORT · HAYWARD, CALIFORNIA

LUcerne 2-5443   TEmplebar 2-7642

June 10, 1956

To Whom It May Concern:

      This is to certify that George W. Flavell has been employed as a Flight Instructor for Fairchild Air Services and California Airways for the past year.

      While in our employ, his services were satisfactory in every manner and I wish to recommend him to anyone who desires to employ him.

              Very truly yours,

              P. J. McManamy
              ATR 340548
              Manager

PJM/p

CHAPTER 4

The First Airlines

ALOHA AIRLINES, Wazu, I am on my way, and in looking back, it was this call and my quick acceptance that were the first big hurdles I jumped. To be getting large aircraft experience this early and at my age was great. In Honolulu in 1957 with a paycheck of $350 a month, I searched for accommodations and found that the only thing I could afford was the YMCA. It was a brand new YMCA on Atkinson's Drive, and I was in a brand new room. I traveled by bus in uniform to and from the airport and learned to chat and take kidding about where my airplane was and to give it back in a good-natured way, which helped me deal with people and passengers in other situations later.

The ground school consisted of DC-3 systems, controls, weight and balance calculations, company radio frequencies, and procedures. The mostly visual routes used between the islands depended on weather and/or seasons. Soon, I felt like an old hand; the captains were letting me have more takeoffs and landings, a sure sign that my copilot duties were okay. On the other hand, it could mean that he has given up on me and has decided to see if I can do anything right. After a string of three grease jobs, the captain moaned, complaining about luck and how it would run out soon. Later, going in to Hilo, on the Big Island, the captain gave me the landing unexpectedly. I had noticed that we were using about 10 degrees of crab on the approach, so I held it. He told me that the crosswind always disappears close to the runway. In close over the island, I started taking out the crab and immediately drifted, so resorting to little airplane tactics I corrected now with a side-slip, and it worked fine, except I had some side-load causing a jolt. Surprisingly, the captain said, "Very good, could have been better if you had not taken out the crab prior to the slip." I replied, "You told me the wind would disappear." "True, but why would you believe that, and worse, you corrected for something that had not happened." "I wanted you to see that I was aware of your warning."

"I'll give you a warning, believe what the aircraft is doing, not what somebody else is telling you, and that goes for the tower or another airplane. It is nice to have a heads-up for some possible event, but let the aircraft you are flying talk to you. Anyhow, you made it harder on yourself than it needed to be. Still a good job."

"OK, I'll take it, and thanks." Later I said, "Do I ever get another landing?" "NO." "I will not pull up the gear anymore." "Good, I won't have to worry about landing with the gear up."

On another trip where it was my leg to fly, the captain started revising his charts and approach plates. I was finishing a cup of tea when our flight attendant came into the cockpit. She was Miss Hawaii for the current year 1957 and would go to the finals in Atlantic City. She asked if I would like some pineapple juice and I said yes. When she returned, we talked about anything I could think of to keep her talking. The captain kept looking sideways at me with a knowing eyebrow. Finishing my pineapple juice, I planned to open my clear-view window, sucking the cup out of my hand. I had seen other pilots do this. This time, it was even more spectacular; the cup along with all the captain's charts and approach plates became a white blizzard for only a second, and then I closed the window. The flight attendant said, "I have to leave now," and left. The captain was busy, putting manuals back in his flight bag. I busied myself, tuning radios and concentrated on flying. In my peripheral vision, I detected his head turned toward me. I quickly glanced over to see how mad he might be. He was waiting for me. His cheeks were puffed out, and he was holding his eyes crossed. The passengers were probably wondering what could be so funny in the cockpit.

I often wondered why the captains refused any pineapple juice because I loved pineapple juice, but after a month of flying, I tired of it also, but I would not quibble about it, if Miss Hawaii was serving.

Because the passenger entry door was all the way in the back of these airplanes, the cockpit crew was in no hurry to get out; in any event, the copilot usually deferred to the captain to go first. On one of our stops, early in my experience, the captain decided to sit in the cockpit until departure time and asked me to pick up the weather from company operations. Walking down the aisle, I ran into a line of passengers who seemed to be deplaning very slowly. In trying to see why, I bent over somewhat to get a better look outside when a middle-age lady (about 35) waiting in front me had the same idea. Our heads came together, and my hat fell off. She reached for it and put it back on my head, albeit crookedly. I, age 24, apologized while she moved her face closer, and in an unnecessarily loud voice said, "I wish you were giving me a lei today," causing much laughter from those around us. I did not understand the situation until I was closer to the door where passenger service was placing flower leis around the neck of each passenger deplaning. The situation, temporarily beyond my comprehension that day, would be better handled now that I have a little black book full of flower shops.

The Islands of Hawaii laid out from the Northwest to the Southeast meant that you were cruising in one of these two general directions. En route were fair weather cumulus clouds. Depending on the time of year, there were occasional rain showers that were usually circumnavigated. There were layovers on the Big Island, Hawaii, at Hilo and

Kona. Body surfing in Kona was spectacular with 10-foot waves and somewhat scary for the uninitiated. Going out was about as difficult as getting in. Getting through the wave without being pitched back and rolled around was the outbound problem. Once on the outside, it was a little unsettling to look toward the beach and see the heavy surf, exploding into the air. Floating around outside of the wave action is beautiful with the volcanic profile of the island and the very fragrance of the air. Each individual has to judge when to start back because there will be moments when holding your breath is necessary. I did not always do it gracefully. Returning to the beach, I have fallen off high breaking waves into water only two or three feet deep, then before gaining my footing pulled by extremely fast outgoing water that is feeding the same wave dragging me up into it and tumbling out of control. Pushed onto the sand in shallow water, I had to gain movement inland very quickly before the cycle started again. Just the thought of facing waves three times that high located on the North Shore of Oahu boggles the mind.

There were other layovers where we would join another crew and go to a beautiful lagoon with overhanging palms and tropical plants. A waterfall was spilling into all of this as well. I mentioned that this looked like a movie setting and learned that it had been many times.

The flight experience I gained with this position was invaluable for future positions. Most candidates apply to airlines with degrees and other formal education, but when the hiring decisions are made, experience weighs in very heavily. Experience is valuable for any skilled position, but logging of actual experience of large airline aircraft in airline operation is not possible. The initial experience is therefore a sort of "Catch-22."

The time was drawing near when I would leave. Others, like me, would return year after year until a full-time job was accrued by seniority. I planned to find something more stable right away.

Flying back to Philadelphia for a visit with my parents, I planned to contact all of the airlines that were flying DC-3s.

ALLEGHENY AIRLINES, Washington, DC, said that the *Airline Guide*, a book published frequently, kept flight times and destinations current. It also had the office numbers for different departments with the names of the individuals. I noted one, the Chief Pilot.

On the phone with Captain Harvey Thompson, I quickly got to my subject. "Sir, I am current and qualified with Aloha Airlines as a DC-3 Copilot; it was a temporary summer job that is over, and I am looking for something new and more stable. I have about 150 hours in the DC-3." Captain Thompson replied, "Son, we have filled a class starting Monday next week. I wish you had called sooner. There is no one in that class with DC-3 experience." I explained that I had just returned two days ago, and he replied, "I can't encourage you to do this, but if you want to, be here on Monday and talk with me; there is always a chance someone will not show up." I told him I would try to do that.

Early Monday morning, after driving half the night, I arrived at the Allegheny Airlines business office that was part of a large hangar area at Washington National Airport. Going inside, I found a reception area where a PBX operator was hard at work. She nodded to me as I approached her desk, at least I thought she had, it was hard to tell since she was so animated. At once smiling and light voiced, then quickly all business. Her voice and her body movements were seemingly controlled by a third party; a wink and a finger movement seemed to be for me but I could not be sure. On one occasion, she would be almost angry with someone then suddenly change the tone of her voice laughing. It was fascinating to watch while every once and a while her eyes would meet mine, yet her words were for someone else. Finally, my hypnotic spell was broken by the words, "Can I help you?" being repeated firmly. "Oh, ahh, yes," I said, "I am supposed to see Captain Thompson." She was gone again, pulling cords, twisting levers, saying, "Good Morning" and "I'll connect you." My absurd sense of humor was starting to surface, a dangerous thing when comportment for an interview is everything. I idly wondered if she could be capable of sex in addition to performing her PBX function. I studied her closely now, thinking of what positions would be possible under those parameters without disturbing her puppet-like functions. She was nicely endowed, from what I could see, and I moved slightly to get a better look at her lower extremities. "Are you a pilot?" she said, breaking my concentration. "Yes," I said as quickly as I could find my voice. She seemed relieved somehow; perhaps my face had reflected my studious thoughts. A slight smile crossed her face, and then she proceeded very business-like and said, "Upstairs, room 204." I glanced back briefly before the door closed behind me, and she was looking at me and smiling, but of course, she was so fickle, you could not trust her smiles, words or actions. Our relationship ended there.

Remembering what had happened when I saw the sign that said *Learn to Fly*, I wondered what room 204 held for me. Through the glass portion of the door, I saw what was probably the pilot class, which had not started yet, since I was very early. I went in thinking that an instructor might be close by who could direct me to the chief pilot's office. Instead, one by one, the others started introducing themselves as did I, and we were still talking when the instructor came in and directed us to take any seat at the various tables. I raised my hand to ask him where I could find Captain Thompson; however, I was directed to a seat as he said, "There will be a time for questions." I sat down. A yellow legal tablet was passed around to be filled out with name, address, contact phone, etc. I presumed that my being on that list would finally bring attention to my situation, but for now, I would at least have not missed any of the required Ground School, which would be an asset regardless.

The days went by and I discovered who were the ones with the most knowledge and experience. They all had my experience and some a little more; of course, this being my second airline and DC-3 background, as little as it was, left me as the resident know-it-all, a title not to be enjoyed and easily destroyed if you were truly to believe it. Pilots that share their experiences and knowledge willingly and helpfully are the respected members of the fraternity; those who play "one-upmanship" are usually weak in confidence, knowledge, or character. As the days went on, I found my seat partner to be weak in several areas, and I worked with him as best I could. He had told me that he really knew ADF procedures and navigation solutions but knew very little about a new system called VOR. I helped him with the VOR, only to find out he knew very little about ADF. I helped him the best I could, but he lived in the area, and so did not stay in the hotel with the rest of us, where time could have been used for helping him. It is a tough business, and maybe he had personal commitments at home that could not be ignored.

Two weeks later, after all the instruction and tests were completed, Captain Thompson came into the room. He congratulated everyone and said, "I would like to call your names out, and if you will raise your hand, I will be able to reacquaint your name with the face." As he went through the list, I waited for this moment; it had been a gamble but the system had not caught me yet. If I lost, it was at my own expense. The others were not paid for their expenses either. Captain Thompson now came to the end of the list and said, "Is there anyone I missed?" I raised my hand, and he asked me my name. He looked again at his list, and then he appeared to be comparing it with the instructor's, finally talking to the instructor in a low voice that could not be heard. The instructor was nodding his head in what I hoped was referring to my performance. Suddenly, he looked up and smiling said, "Welcome aboard." I then had to fill out an employment application. We were all going to be flying for Allegheny Airlines, out of Pittsburgh, Pennsylvania. Thank you, Ms. PBX.

After arriving in Pittsburgh and establishing my living quarters, I reported to the Pittsburgh chief pilot's office. The others gradually showed up, and we awaited our fate. It was rumored that the Pittsburgh chief pilot, Captain Pete Petrie, would be taking us flying for flight evaluations. We were sent out on the ramp to wait for the captain. A DC-3 was parked close by.

Captain Petrie finally showed up and told us how we would all get a chance to fly the airplane and we better be good because the airline didn't waste any time on people needing basic training. "Now, where is the guy with all the DC-3 time?" he said. At this point, I raised my hand and started to remind him that I did not have much, but he cut me off. "Get in the cockpit and get strapped in, but don't touch anything; the rest of you get in aisle seats close to the cockpit, and when we are airborne, you can stand forward and observe silently." The steep aisle of the DC-3 being a tail wheel airplane is consciously noticeable. Climbing into the copilot seat was probably one of the few things that I had down pat; as you straddled the yoke in front of the seat, you automatically fell into it. As I looked around, most everything was the same except for the flexible medal tube that carried heat to the cockpit when it was turned on, something that was certainly not installed or needed in the Aloha DC-3s.

Petrie launched into the cockpit still shouting to those in the back about one thing or another, regarding observing the cockpit and the candidate flying at the time. All it meant to me was that I would not have the advantage of watching someone else go first. I mentioned to Captain Petrie that I did not have any charts or even know the radio frequencies of the Pittsburgh Airport. "Just sit still, and I'll get us going." He handled the engine starting and taxied out, all the while handling the radios too. Once on the regular taxiway, he asked me, "Can you taxi the aircraft all right?" "Yes I can," I answered and put the tail wheel lock on. He promptly took it off saying, "Anyone can taxi straight with that on; let me see you taxi without it." I had to drag a little brake on one side to straighten it out, and then used differential power to hold us straight. He complained about the brake use. When we got close to the runway, he switched to tower, finished the checklist himself, did a quick runup and mag check, and told me to start the takeoff as soon as we got on the runway. I reminded him that we had not gotten clearance on the runway. He smiled and called in ready and the tower cleared us for takeoff. Once on the runway I brought up the outside (of the turn) engine a little, and then balanced it with the other before bringing them up to the suggested manifold pressure. He immediately started screaming, "Keep it straight; you're going to lose it this way, more right rudder." I did not see the need for anything he was talking about and flew it out, determined to fail on my own terms. He had not overridden any of my inputs, so maybe he was trying to distract me. We did some air work and such, and then headed back toward Pittsburgh. When we were on a heading to intercept the localizer of the ILS, and the needle had just begun to move, he said, "I am out of cigarettes, you got any?" I had some in my pocket where they were clearly visible, but I said no and turned the airplane sharply to capture the needle correctly. After finding the heading to keep the needle centered, I pulled my cigarettes out and offered them to him. He said, "Thanks, I don't smoke." The glide-slope needle came into view, and when it was centered, I called for the landing gear down and reduced the power somewhat to follow the slope to the runway. He pulled the power back on the left engine at the same time calling out, "Engine failure." The aircraft yawed to the left, and I caught it with the right rudder and re-trimmed the aircraft

36

while calling for the engine failure checklist. He said, "I can't find the checklist; what are you going to do?" I said, "Feather the left engine." "It's simulated feathered," he responded. I reached for the right prop control, and he asked, "What do you want?" "I want to move the prop to low pitch and then apply more power." "How much more power?" I said, "Maximum Continuous." "It is simulated set at Maximum Continuous," he replied. The airspeed was falling off fast. Clearly, I would not be able to stay on the glide path, I said, "I am going to push the throttle to the firewall if I have to." "That is what I want to hear, now take the throttle back and you have two engines, I will roll out your rudder trim."

When that day ended, we were all signed off to go out and fly the line as an observer. Sitting in the jump seat, in between and slightly behind the pilots, the actual procedures, checklists, radio frequencies and in-flight operations were observed and notations made. Flight conditions permitting questions and answers would occur in real time. Later, on the ground between ourselves, each one's experience is talked about, hoping always to get a greater edge on survival whether it is aviation technology or getting employed. Watching the interaction of a crew at work assists us in grasping the duties and flow of how each will have to perform when put in that position. One of our classmates was not signed off at this time, and later we learned he was not accepted. His nickname was "Steb," and he was a very personable and funny guy. He had kept our morale up as we went through ground school and flight reviews. I, however, knew that he was weak in many things in ground school because he had sat next to me. When he would whisper a question, I would move my paper over where he could see my answer. After all, I felt the airline profession catches all weaknesses at some level. He later failed due to a lack of knowledge with "Morse Code." All of us were sad; he had risked two weeks and much more; he loved flying. It is a risky business in many ways, always demanding of knowledge, health, flying skills, flexibility of lifestyle regarding flight schedules, days off, base domiciles, not to mention initial low pay and forfeit of some days off for re-current ground schools and many other responsibilities. On a scale of novice to airline pilot, Steb was 90% there for the job he was applying for. He struck out; 90% is not passing. I hope he fixed his problems, because down through my career I tried to avoid being like Steb. The thought of him helped me to study harder; he reminded me that 90% could be a failing grade, and I knew about failing grades.

My first line trip assignment as First Officer (Copilot) was with Captain Bearclaw, although that is not the way it was spelled; that was the way it was pronounced.

I busied myself, collecting the weather information along with the various other papers and was busy reviewing for the 100th time the sequence of things I had to do when I got in the aircraft. Suddenly I heard Captain Bearclaw being paged by company dispatch, and I moved over towards that area to see if he responded. As he walked up to the counter, I heard the crew scheduler tell him he had a new copilot today and mentioned my name. Looking at him at that moment, I hoped that I could look that sharp when I became a captain. After several weeks of flying with him, I only wished that I could fly as well. A prince of a guy, he was full of helpful advice and freely let me fly almost every other leg. One day, walking to the airplane early, I noticed a baggage handler having trouble putting a large bag in the rear belly. As he was alone, I went over and gave him a hand. Afterward as I was doing a pre-flight walk-around, another Allegheny captain came over to me and chewed me out for helping the baggage handler. When I started to defend myself, he got hot. Just then, I noticed Bearclaw coming along, and so did this other pilot. "Ugh, hi bear, just telling your copilot here to keep his hands off the baggage." Bearclaw turned to me and said smiling, "Keep your hands off the baggage," then turned to the other pilot and said,

"How's that?" The other pilot said, "Uh well you know how it is and…" Bearclaw interrupted and said, "You flying this airplane today?" "Uh no well…" "Then this must be my airplane, is that right?" He said, "Yup, you are right, sorry, you have a good trip." He left a little humbled and Bearclaw laughed, and then apologized for the other pilot, saying, "He really is right, but he handles it wrong. We had a contract clause once that said the pilots had to help load baggage. It was an old section, and we had the devil to pay to get rid of it so that is what the history is. The last part has to do with personality differences where he once stood up in a meeting and said that each pilot should fly his own damn airplane and quit trying to dictate to others how to do it. Therefore, I reminded him that this is my airplane, which left him defenseless according to his own principles. However, he is good at heart and a good pilot. I would suggest you apologize to him the next time you see him. No point in hard feelings particularly when you are new, regardless of how poorly he handled it." That turned out to be good advice, as later I would fly with that captain and enjoyed his friendship and the many improvements to my flying skills that he taught me.

My instrument flying was honed with Allegheny Airlines because they made many approaches, particularly non-directional radio beacons (NDB). The routes I flew from Pittsburgh went to Phillipsburg, Lock Haven, Williamsport, Harrisburg and Atlantic City. There were others; I think Bradford, Erie, Scranton, Hagerstown MD were also in the route structure. I remember that the nonstop Pittsburgh to Atlantic City only operated in the summer, and the flight cruised at the nosebleed altitude of 4000 or 5000 feet.

During consecutive days of flying and remaining overnight (RON) away from Pittsburgh, the company paid for hotels, but if I returned to my home base of Pittsburgh, I would be on my own. I would overnight in the layover crew room. It appeared to have been a meeting room converted to double

WASHINGTON NATIONAL AIRPORT, WASHINGTON 1, D.C.

April 22, 1959

Mr. George W. Flavell
California Airways
Municipal Airport
Hayward, California

Dear George:

This is to advise you that effective May 1, 1959 we will
have a recall of pilots for a period of four (4) months,
approximate.

Would you please advise me if you will be available for
recall at this time, or just how soon, if at all, you
would be available.

It is necessary that I inform you that due to the length
of time you have been on Leave of Absence, if you do not
wish to return to schedule for this recall we will have
no recourse but to remove your name from the Pilot's
Seniority List.

Please advise us as soon as possible of your intentions.

Sincerely yours,

Harvey M. Thompson
Director of Operations

bunk beds, just like the barracks on the ship. The main purpose was for the airline crews to have somewhere to relax when their transit time between trips was too short to pay for a hotel room but long enough to take a nap or relax. For anyone wanting to overnight, there was a nominal charge. To avoid having to pay for this, I would bid a line trip that flew a short leg out of Pittsburgh to Huntington, West Virginia. It immediately went into an overnight layover on arrival and flew out again early in the morning back to Pittsburgh. This "RON" was not popular with crew members based and living in Pittsburgh. I would bid or cover these trips whenever I could, saving money and getting a company-paid hotel room for the night.

This experience with Allegheny Airlines was to benefit me greatly in several ways. One was the experience of the DC-3 itself, in all kinds of weather, flying with pilots who had years of experience and had been with the company as it had grown. Their style of cockpit management was different from the other, which is not conducive for copilots who had to keep notes on the priorities of each captain. It was a wealth in its own way though because it was not that some were right or wrong but varied the manner, timing or use of things that work. Broad experiences thrived, each being safe and based on actual experience. In those days (1957), pilots resented and resisted speed adjustments and/or heading assignments given by the Air Traffic Controllers. Their attitude was "You are not getting in my cockpit" or "flying my airplane." The ATC system was changing. Bigger and faster, four engine DC-7s, Lockheed Super Constellations, Boeing Strata-cruisers and the new Turbo-prop jets, like the British Viscounts, were mixing with slower DC-3s and other even lighter and slower aircraft. For the ATC system was based on first come, first served, accept a Heading, Speed, or Hold. My Allegheny days were numbered. Four months will not fit my goal. My new plan was the non-skeds, four engines, international flying. If only I could make it happen.

CHAPTER 5

Back to the Minor League

One of the biggest changes for me in 1958 was to be furloughed (laid off but with rights of recall based on seniority). It actually was our entire class. A recession was still haunting the country, particularly in the East. I had gone to Wings Field in Ambler, Pennsylvania, looking for charter or flight instructing work and found a little but not enough to live on.

I finally found work with the "Keystone Automobile Club." It was riding a Harley Davidson Motorcycle on road patrol. We would assist any cars stalled or out of gas to get moving again; this would be free for members and I think we charged nonmembers but only for gas, which still encouraged membership. We rode with black leather jackets and white helmets, similar to the Philadelphia police, which made it easier to patrol since we got a little courtesy from the traffic out of doubt about our identity. It paid fifty dollars a week, and at least two of us had to really talk to be hired. They were suspicious of two of us; one had just got out of the service as a submariner and me as an airline pilot. We both had to convince the hiring manager that we were never going to follow those career paths again. I am not even sure he believed we were what we said we were anyhow. It was fun for the month I worked, but I found a lead to a flight instructor job in Flushing, New York, and left. The job in New York was not worth my effort, and I soon realized I had to get back to California. I called Harper Aviation, and they said I could come back as a flight instructor. I accepted, but I needed to get there. I called a friend, a Piper dealer in Palo Alto, California, who had instructed me for my Multi-Engine

Rating. He told me I could ferry a new aircraft from the Piper factory in Lock Haven, Pennsylvania, back to him if the price was right. I told him I would do it for nothing, but it was take it or leave it. He said he would not quibble because of our friendship. I called him a liar, and we had a deal. I delivered a newly named and designed Piper Comanche 180 to Palo Alto, California, finding out along the way during fuel stops that this might be the first delivery going to California. It turned out to be the second.

Now back in California I headed to San Carlos, back from the airlines, back to where I know this flying business is dangerous. The real danger is starving to death. Since I wanted to fly the big iron with the airlines, they used to kid me about having "Four Fan Fever," but I have only been successful chasing two fan aircraft so far, but I am not through yet.

Reid Saindon greets me. Reid was an accountant in San Francisco when I first met him. He used to ride the bus to downtown San Carlos and walk over to the San Carlos Airport and Harper Aviation for lessons. He had a commercial license but wanted a flight instructor rating. He had already failed once using an off the street flight instructor. Frank Celestries, the chief pilot, had briefed me about his flying history and wanted to give him to me. Apparently, he would not follow Frank's instructions, and Frank was disgusted with him. I took over and convinced Reid that if he follows what I do and what I tell him, he will pass. All went well and I asked him if he wanted a job instructing. He asked if I had that authority, and I told him no and that Frank certainly will resist, but I thought I could influence Hap Harper. Frank's problem was that he was too fatherly with his students, which worked for the young and the old, though delaying normal progress. He was also reluctant to do full breaking stalls and spins needed among other semi-acrobatic maneuvers for the flight instructor rating. Making sure that I did not injure a friendship with Frank, I managed to get Reid hired. I had sold Hap on the idea that since we needed another instructor that Reid would be ideal, freshly trained, and doing things our way. Besides, he will be grateful, loyal, and unable to find as good a flying job so quickly. Reid turned out to be a good instructor, plus he was well organized, and the school needed a better curriculum that he designed and had approved by the CAA.

Reid and I walked over to the coffee shop together, and I asked him why he was wearing a suit since the instructors all had uniforms. It is all your fault; you hired me and now I am a vice-president of the corporation. What corporation? Where is Hap Harper? Oh not to worry; he is the president and CEO; many things are going on since you left. Who runs the flight school? Well, I have that as one of my chores, and I will keep an eye on it, but I want you to be Chief Flight Instructor, but no one knows that yet. If you agree, I will talk to Hap. OK with me.

Dusty Rhoads came over, putting out his newly wiped off hand and said, "Glad to see you back." After bringing us coffees, Dusty mentioned that I could even order a "side order of bacon" with a tomato and lettuce sandwich anytime I wanted. "What is that all about?" asked Reid, after Dusty turned and walked away. It had to do with his painted prices on the smoke hood over the grill. He repainted them one day as I was sitting at the counter talking to him and somehow, sharp as he is with a nickel, I noticed that it was cheaper to buy a "Lettuce and Tomato Sandwich" with a side order of bacon than it was to order a "BLT." Of course the next time I ordered my favorite sandwich I changed it to just a Lettuce and Tomato sandwich. He asked me if I was tired of bacon and I said no. A minute later, I asked for a side order of bacon, and he cheerfully said, "Right away, I will slide it into your sandwich." "No," I said. "I will just bring it over to you." "I want the side order plate, please." He got quiet, and he, not smiling, brought it over with a napkin under the dish and told me that I could not have it served that way again. He stared at me as I took the sandwich apart and placed the bacon on it, and then chomping furiously on the crunchy bacon, I mumbled, "How you going…to stop me?" "I just will not serve it." "How 'bout I order the bacon first? Suppose I order two eggs over with toast, slice of tomato and lettuce and side of bacon." "You're a real pain in the ass, ya know." I agreed. "He is a funny duck," said Reid, then getting right down to business, he outlined the plans that Hap had for the airport. There would be a parent company created which would own the airport itself; everything else would be treated as a concession, wholly owned or otherwise. "Whew sounds like the money is coming from somewhere other than aviation, is it?" "In a way yes, but the attraction is aviation. We have two aircraft dealerships now, and a pending third plus a Uniflite boat dealership. We plan to own the airport and the T-Hangers, the fuel concession and a ferryboat." "A ferryboat, now that is something I might like to check out on, but tell me about the three aircraft dealerships." "Well we have Cessna, Mooney, and soon we should have Colonial Skimmer, an amphibian seaplane." "I know a lot about Cessna, but I have never heard of Mooney or the last one." "Mooney is not particularly new but is being improved. They are based in Kerrville, Texas, and right now, they have two aircraft models. The Mooney Mark 18 and the Mooney Mark 20 both have retractable landing gear. We are going to have one in the "Cow Palace" Boat Show in South San Francisco next month. Harper thinks he will sell some there. What is the downside to this aircraft, Reid? I sense something in your voice. It has a wooden wing spar, George. I thought they quit doing that years ago. All right, George, go easy, this is a very serious matter with Hap; he is somewhat stressed because of so many things coming together. We have people from the Hacienda in Las Vegas helping us to go public with the company, and this information is very secret, so for now just listen and do not engage in any conversations with anyone but me or Hap. As far as Mooney Aircraft Corporation, it is a big opportunity for us; we could become a distributor instead of just a dealership. For now, George, let us go over the flight school details and then I want to introduce you to some new instructors that I know you have not met.

Everything Reid talked about was taking place around us, and then one day Reid walked in and told me we were going to buy a Twin Beech D-18. He asked me if I ever flew one, and I had not, but I offered that the rumors about that airplane were legendary. Tricky to handle and ground looping are always the things mentioned. Reid decided that Dave Penny, one of our instructors, who had military experience flying them, should be the delivery pilot.

We would go along. It was a rebuilt military model put together by a Trans-Ocean Airlines mechanic who had a private license but did not want to fly it. We insisted he come along and fly in the copilot seat if we were to buy it, and he did. Once airborne, they did some air work with it, and then headed across the bay from Oakland to San Carlos Airport. When the mechanic saw the short field length of the San Carlos Airport, he became nervous. About this same time, the oil temp gauge began to show high on the left engine. Dave, our pilot, looked a little warm himself. I suggested pulling the power back on that engine to see if the temperature would decrease. Dave did, and it soon came into the green again. We approached the field to land with the power reduced on the left engine. We came in and were just inches from the ground when Dave decided to go around.

I did not know what the minimum control speed was for that aircraft with an engine out, but I knew of no other aircraft with an engine out that would have been able to reach that point on the runway and go around without crashing. I shouted, "Bring the left engine power in," and Dave jumped, but put the power on, stopping a slow turn to the left that would have ended in a snap-roll into the ground. We came around for another approach. The ex-owner in the copilot's seat offered to get out, but I told him to stay there that Dave was the best pilot I knew for this job and to just stay away from the controls. I told Dave to do the best job he could do but to put it on the runway this time, no matter what. "It will not have to be a grease job, and you will just do fine, and if you're too fast to stop before the end, just force it to ground loop." Dave did an acceptable job this time, but everyone was relieved to be on the ground.

When we went into the office, Reid said, "What do you think?" I said, "I think we should learn to fly it." No kidding, we bought it; we have to learn to fly it, but who can we get right now to fly it? That is my question. You are not paying attention. I said <u>we</u>. You mean you and me. Yup, you and me. Reid paused, "When you taught me to be a flight instructor, had you ever done that before?" "No," I said, "but you were a good student." "And you are a good liar," said Reid. Do you really think we can go out there and get proficient, in say a week? Absolutely. You are sure? Would I lie to you? I hope so if that is what makes it work. Reid had the Twin Beech taken into the maintenance hangar and gone over by "Cookie," our guy in charge. He had found the problem with the oil temperature and a few others, then blessed the beast for another 100 hours.

During the next three days, we learned a lot from that airplane as we compensated for all the folklore stories about it. When we stopped anticipating all the special problems told about it and then relaxed and flew it like any other airplane, things improved greatly. It was like thinking you were going to ride a bad horse only to find that you got on the wrong one that was already trained and all you had to do was let the beast do its thing. One thing, however, was to pay attention taxiing and not to get that tail swinging around fast with differential power or other hotshot tricks or it would show some of its own.

Some of the other instructors had been checked out on it now, and it was doing some charters to Reno and Lake Tahoe.

The Mooney Dealership was inked, and it was not long before we had a Mooney Mark-20 and a Mooney Mite-18, which was a lot of fun. The Mite was as close to a single place fighter aircraft as I ever came—fast and responsive in power, smooth flight controls and you had to slow it down in the traffic pattern if the Cessnas were around and all of this on a 65 Hp Continental Engine.

Reid had an idea to park it near the office frontage to attract private pilots going by on Highway 101, which ran close by. It did not appear to generate much interest. One morning coming to work, I was driving behind one of the office secretaries whose pickup truck had a western saddle on a rack in the bed of the truck. After parking, I told her what I wanted to do and she said okay. I put the saddle on the fuselage between the cockpit canopy and the tail section and parked it near a sign that said "Scenic Rides." That brought quite a bit of interest, all wanting to watch someone go for a ride, not go themselves. When someone put a child in the saddle, I quickly did away with that idea before the aircraft was damaged.

The Mark-20 that also had a Laminar Flow wing design gave it a good speed increase over many similar aircraft. It was a retractable gear aircraft but with human power. A long bar with a sleeve-type collar allowed your hand to grasp it in a backhanded upside down (thumb to floor) way. Pressing down on the collar would unlatch the bar loose from a locking latch and to move it ninety degrees to the floor in one motion where it would latch again, in the gear retracted position now. It was an interesting operation and quite amusing. As you unlocked it from the vertical position, the bar had immediate weight to it that wanted to drive it toward the floor and you must be ready to assist that force to be able to quickly get it to the floor and latched. The exact reverse takes place in the gear extension process. The important thing is to remember that there is a lot of weight that wants to take the bar to the halfway position. That is the reason for moving quickly, taking advantage of the initial momentum to assist you in moving the bar all the way. As an example of not doing it properly, it will stop at the mid position. If this happens, it can be solved by moving the bar a little in either direction and getting a little pendulum effect started, until you can assist it to the full up or down position.

With the Twin Beech now in service, we were flying more charters to Reno and Lake Tahoe, and we had enough pilots checked out in it but now had to hire a couple of more flight instructors.

The San Carlos Airport was a 2600-foot runway and surrounded by tidal water sloughs from the San Francisco Bay. This water access is what led Hap Harper to buy the "Klamath" ferryboat that used to ply the Sacramento River. It was towed over to a basin that had been prepared for it on the airport property. After getting it into position in the basin, a cofferdam was built and the basin flooded and maintained by pumps to an acceptable and permanent height. Workers were all over it, ripping out some bulkheads, installing others not quite so seaworthy and installing plumbing and kitchen equipment. The plan was to refurbish it into a gourmet restaurant including a hotel and business convention center. Suggestions for an appropriate name for the hotel were solicited, with a yet unknown prize for the winner. I won the name game but never saw a prize. The name I submitted was "Chandelle Inn," the first being an aviation acrobatic name.

Professional stock salespeople were raising all of the money necessary and earning money in the process. We had some employees who quit to join the sales force.

Our Twin Beech advertising helped promote the Reno and Lake Tahoe flights and attracted some aviation interests who owned a scheduled Air Taxi operation they wanted to sell.

Golden Gate Airways operated flights between San Francisco International Airport and Travis Air Force Base, about 45 minutes between the two. The parties owned the small airline and the travel agency that sold the tickets. All of this was under the "Airline Transport Association" of American. The ATA ticket stock was printed in accordance with the rules and regulations of that institution. Collections of money were balanced on a monthly basis to reflect reconciliation of earned fares.

The above information translates to a huge cash flow favoring Golden Gate Airways. A military passenger arriving at Travis AFB from overseas buys a ticket to New York on <u>GGA</u> Ticket Stock. The ticket will show as follows:

<u>GGA</u>:

FROM: SUU TO: SFO $ 75.00

<u>UAL:</u>

FROM: SFO TO: JFK $ 250.00

There were no other operations in the country quite like this. The sellers were interested in retiring, and Hap Harper purchased the company. For me this meant a choice of staying with the school or going to San Francisco as Chief Pilot of GGA. Since they were flying Twin Beech D-18s, I went with GGA. This was in July 1960.

We were going to keep all of the employees both at Travis and San Francisco, but about half the pilots wanted to quit when they met me. I could understand their feelings. I was 28 years of age and looked younger; all of them were 10 to 20 years older and were used to working for a much more experienced pilot. Of the ones that wanted to leave, I convinced half of them to give me a chance. I told them the company was behind me and that was not going to change in case they were thinking otherwise. I told them I would respect their experience and where questions or differences existed, my door was open, along with my mind. I also told them I could fly the D-18 and that I would do some flying, checking and standardizing of procedures, along with their inputs. As I made progress along these lines, I found that Hap wanted to get a DC-3 for charters to Reno and Elko, Nevada. This was filled with complications because we would have to deal with two different sections of the FAA. One would be the "General Aviation Offices" for aircraft weighing less than 12,500 lbs, which is everything we had been doing, but the DC-3 is twice that weight and would fall under "Air Carrier Operations."

That would mean that a pilot flying a Beech D-18 would have to do a check ride once a year in that aircraft to stay qualified for the General Aviation Office, and if we had him dual qualified, he would have to do another check ride in a DC-3 to qualify for the Air Carrier Office.

I explained all of that to Reid. I also mentioned that we would have to have a Chief Pilot for the DC-3 because I am not a qualified "Pilot In Command" in that aircraft. Further, even if I was, I did not have enough flight time in "Heavy Aircraft," defined as greater than 12,500 lbs. Reid said he would think it over and work something out.

The next time I met with Reid, there were several changes. A new parent company, "Cal-West Inc.," was the parent company of Harper Aviation and Golden Gate Airways and of many other newly formed subsidiaries such as the Ferry Boat, Hotel, Airport, Hangars, Fuel Concession, Uniflite Boats, Cessna, Mooney, Aircraft Repair and Radio Shop.

Position changes were Hap Harper as President and CEO of Cal-West and Reid as Senior Vice President of Harper Aviation and President of Golden Gate Airways. I would become Director of Operations of Golden Gate Airways and Chief Pilot of Travis Operations.

A Chief Pilot to be in charge of DC-3 Operations would be hired. Oh, to be back to being a real airline pilot again and to get away from this minor league! Everyone seemed to be upbeat about how this was going, but all I ever wanted to do was to fly. My four-fan fever goal had been right all along. I was wasting time. The DC-7 was calling me, and I never got a foot in the door. ONA was the cream of the crop in the non-skeds, hard to be hired, but real pros flying worldwide. Quit whining, I told myself. I was lucky to have a job. I started interviewing candidates for the DC-3 Chief Pilot job.

Older guys would come in and tell me how much DC-3 time they had and with no logbooks or references. Then Jack showed up, and he knew everything, flew everything, could handle the FAA, knew the regulations and was personable in a controlling sort of way. Experience was his forte and lack thereof in this manner was mine, yet my instinct was aroused. He could be a perfect pilot and be a poor fit into our operation. I decided to sleep on it. The next day I realized that part of my doubt was caused by my position. The FAA would see me in a weak position as Chief Pilot of the D-18 fleet only and not in their jurisdiction. The title Director of Operations does not require a pilot license and is not an officer of the company, sort of a nonentity as pertains to Jack's territory. I mentioned to Reid about the situation of Jack and the FAA working together without oversight from the company's perspective, trying to get Reid involved. I suggested that I could brief him on any issues that needed to be addressed and hoped he would see the need. Instead, he promoted me to Vice President Flight Operations with notification to the FAA that nothing was final without my approval.

Jack's attitude changed remarkably, but I did not take pleasure in that sort of office politics. Getting into the cockpit again was my idea of progress. I worried that the DC-7 was getting old, and soon they would be replaced with Jets, and the likely chance of my getting a chance to fly a four-engine jet was about as likely as going to the moon.

The choice of a DC-3 boiled down to two that were for sale. One was a high performing modified aircraft that met transport quality performance, known as T-Category. I bought this aircraft—well above average in condition with manuals and performance charts and all the things that seemed right. I selected that and found a complex issue.

The complex issue was very simple: if it had never been improved and certified as T-Category, it would be grandfathered in without question. Having manuals and performance graphs, we would have to limit our weights to meet that new criteria for all airports we would use. The end result was that we had a better, more powerful and safer airplane, but could not compete with one that had not been improved and certified. As it turned out, we did not really have competition.

We also were doing very well with charters to Reno and Elko, Nevada. Lake Tahoe was out of the question with our DC-3, but we still operated the Twin Beech D-18s into the Tahoe Valley Airport. TWA had tried operating in there

GEORGE W. FLAVELL
DIRECTOR OF OPERATIONS

GOLDEN GATE AIRWAYS
EXECUTIVE TERMINAL
INTERNATIONAL AIRPORT   JUno 9-1713

Golden Gate
AIRWAYS

GEORGE W. FLAVELL
Vice-President

Executive Terminal
San Francisco International Airport   •   JUno 9-1713

before but had given it up. They had purchased and installed station radios and contracted with Airinc to be able to handle the required communications from the Tahoe office to arriving and departing aircraft. At that time, the airport did not have a tower or any weather-reporting facilities. After checking that there were no conflicting "three letter airport designations" that would conflict with my choice of "TVL" for the Tahoe Airport, which was located in Tahoe Valley, I used that Airport Identifier on the baggage tags as well as the ticket receipts that we used in lieu of ATA tickets on the D-18 operations. The FAA said we could not use them until we received approval from ICAO. I thought this was a non-item, and so I told them we had verbal approval. They did not believe it. To this day, I do not know what occurred, but later, all concerned got letters from ICAO indicating Lake Tahoe was "TVL."

The DC-3 operation and the D-18 scheduled airline lasted almost two years and then the parent company fell on bad times, some inherent flaw in their business plan that drew us into the problem. Finally, as the paychecks stopped coming, we had to close the doors. I found a job at a machine shop running a turret lathe. I told them I was a machinist, but they either did not believe it or did not care. I had forgotten most of the nomenclature for all the tools and things you need to check out of the tool crib, so it was probably the former. One day, I broke a tool bit, and I ground a new one. When they discovered I could do that, I got a raise. Later they saw me adjusting the length of a stroke on one of the turret positions and gave me another raise. I received another raise when I volunteered to set up a complete run on the turret lathe and then did it; the week after that I quit. When they asked me why, I told them it takes too long to get a raise around here, but then I told them what was good news for me. I had a chance to become a pilot with "Overseas National Airways." "You ever fly before?" they asked. "A little," I replied.

CHAPTER 6

Four Fan Fever

I really did not have a job yet, just a chance to sit in ground school for two weeks. If they did not get enough people with four-engine experience by the end of two weeks, I would have a chance to move to flight evaluation. If they had their quota, I could sit in for another two weeks going through ground school again with the same gamble.

There had been three of us in the same boat; one dropped out after the first two weeks, and Bill Timmons and myself became friends after not being accepted and sat through the last gamble. They accepted us both at the end, but only to go to flight evaluation. There were 14 pilot applicants waiting for cockpit time as we flew around the Bay area. Each would do an ILS approach to a landing, and then make a touch and go.

There would be another two of the same before the next pilot got in the seat. I was next to last with Bill Timmons to follow. Steedman Hinckley was the flight instructor and captain on this flight. He had the Type Rating by virtue of assignment to training and could not hold a captain's position on the seniority list.

He was the man to impress on this flight, however. I settled into the seat when it was my turn and found an instrument I had never seen before. Actually, I had seen it in ground school, but, just being a compass, I was not going to ask any questions about such a basic instrument lest I draw attention to my lack of experience on four-engine aircraft. It was an RMI, Remote Magnetic Indicator. It was a simple, straightforward presentation in every way except in making turns, where it rotated just the opposite of the older gyrocompass. It should not have been hard to use, but I was having great difficulty by turning the wrong way initially, and then having to re-bank the opposite way. Captain Hinckley had no idea of what could be wrong since he had been a pilot in the airforce and flown DC-6s for MAC. I am sure he was considering washing me out except for the fact that I could fly well, land well, and did well on the ILS, and I suspected they needed me or I would not have made it.

My first assignment was with Captain Fred Wright. I think he had been briefed by Hinckley because he seemed hesitant to let me fly the airplane during the first two weeks. That helped me in a way to get all my First Officer duties in order. He gradually became more outgoing and started giving me more legs to fly. I managed to resolve my problem with the RMI, but I had a little trouble calling for the power settings. I was used to setting my own power in any aircraft I had flown, and here, the Flight Engineer had that responsibility once the pilot flying called for the specified power. I would have to announce 150 BMEP (Brake Mean Effective Pressure), 2000 RPM (Revolutions Per Minute), and the Engineer would make the adjustment for power and prop pitch. The pilot did handle the power on takeoff and landing. At other times, it was more comfortable when the engineer made the adjustments, considering the passengers' ears and the props staying synchronized better.

The month wore on, and finally Captain Wright said, "I am very proud of myself." "Why?" I asked respectfully. He said, "For making you a very good pilot." "Thank you," I said. I did not want to sound too sincere in case he was kidding, but nothing followed, so I accepted it.

Long quiet flights were punctuated by air traffic control calls, cockpit conversations that wax and wane, flight plan progression reports, and readings of fluids, temperatures and pressures. The Engineer called the captain Fred when speaking conversationally, but "Captain" in response to Tech Talk. I did not feel comfortable enough yet to broach the personal salutation, but I thought it was a good formula to emulate.

We had been out several days now, and the next trip was to Honolulu. We would have a navigator join us now when we made a stop at Oakland. This is what separated ONA from scheduled airlines. The same crews would operate both domestically and internationally, which wasn't always the most efficient for crew or company since they would be restricted to 100 hours of flying a month, using the most restrictive rule which was domestic flying. It did however require everyone to keep passports, shots and international health cards up to date and always with you. The captains carried a company checkbook to pay for anything that came up whether it was fuel, hotel or per diem advance. They also carried a Green ATP Travel Card that would let them buy tickets for a planeload of passengers, if for some reason we were unable to complete our trip. Another example of independent authority for the captain was that he and a dispatcher did not share responsibility for the safe operation of the airplane. ONA had no dispatch center, only flight following, which did just about everything except dispatch. Each inbound captain released the aircraft to an outbound captain just by signing the maintenance log if there were no maintenance write-ups. If there was a write-up, the aircraft was released to maintenance and had to be repaired or entered in a carryover log and the logbook signed off as airworthy, which releases the aircraft to a captain.

Three days later after a layover in Honolulu, we were at the airport getting ready to leave when an FAA agent showed up in dispatch. He introduced himself to all of us and asked for our licenses. Only the captain could not find his, said he must have left it somewhere or other, and went about filing the flight plan. The FAA agent advised him he was not going anywhere without showing him his license. Fred turned and looked at him and told him he had been a district manager of an FAA office in Oklahoma City and that he was way out of line. He indicated if he was truly concerned, he should solicit a message from ONA-JFK, giving him the details he wanted or to contact OAK City. The agent continued to disagree and Fred told him not to be standing too close to those engines when we get ready to start because we are leaving on time.

The engineer and I left to go to the airplane and had most everything ready when the captain arrived. We went through the checklist, and when the checklist called for clearing the engine, I looked out the window and shouted clear just as the agent appeared from under the aircraft and said he was not through checking the aircraft. "Tell him to get out of there and if he is not in the way of Eng #3, finish the checklist." I shouted to clear #3 again, and he moved over by Eng #4 and then I loudly called, "Select 3, Turn 3," and we turned through 12 blades to completely clear all cylinders before turning the magnetos on. The agent looked unhappy, but he was standing at the wing tip now, and as I called 4, 8, 12 and the Mags were turned on, everything disappeared in a cloud of gray-blue smoke and a heavy explosive deep breathing engine sent a whirling huge four-bladed monster propeller into creating a hurricane force behind us.

As the engineer settled the thousands of horsepower into a mere gale force idle, I closed my sliding window and made the same calls for engine #4. The captain made the same calls for engines #2 and #1. The flight engineer handled the throttles, prime and mixtures for all four starts.

I had seen some differences of opinions with the FAA before, but this was a much more interesting brush-off. We were off to Oakland, and I never heard a word about it. I am sure I would have, if any violations had occurred.

Back in Oakland again, I had a couple of days off and then I went out again with Fred. We flew several CAM trips, "Civil Air Movements," for the military. Many of them were for the historic airborne units such as the 82nd Airborne out of Fort Bragg, North Carolina, and 101st Airborne, "Screaming Eagles," out of Fort Campbell, Kentucky.

These airborne troops were always running, it seemed. They would board the aircraft like it was leaving in 30 seconds. All knew their seat assignments because there was no wasted time from the moment they arrived until the doors closed. They even loaded their own baggage into the belly cargo compartments from waiting trucks. Both of these flights went to other bases in the U.S. If they had destinations outside the U.S., they would not be considered a CAM.

Returning to Oakland from the CAM flight on October 15, 1962, I found a furlough notice in my company mailbox. A number of others were also affected.

I kept the DC-7 "Technique Manual" which had been written by ONA. It described all the maneuvers including a Canyon Descent and Missed Approach, as well as all calls and power settings for particular phases of flight. It was constructed to take you through an FAA "Type Rating" Ride in the most efficient way.

What a sputtering way to success, if in fact I would be successful—time to find work again.

It was not long in coming; the next morning, ONA called me and said the furlough was cancelled indefinitely, and I was told to pack for at least 30 days and to standby for assignment. "The Cuban Missile Crisis" was in full bloom. The next phone call ordered me to Oakland to ferry a DC-7 to England Air Force Base in Alexandria, Louisiana. ONA had fourteen DC-7s, and at least half of them were operating between England AFB and Savanna, Georgia. We were parked on the civilian side of the field where a small fixed base operator had the fuel concession. Where before he handled fuel octane ranging from 80 to 100 octane, he now used every means possible to deliver the 115-145 octane needed for the DC-7s.

The picture still in my memory is of two men in bib overhauls, straw hats, standing on the top of each wing, holding the fuel nozzles while near the front of each wing stood two 1200 gallon trucks alternately connected for continuous pumping or returning to be filled themselves. The remaining memory is of one of these men shouting to the other, "Look yonder, another one coming." As I turned, I saw they were looking eastward where another ONA DC-7 was returning from Savannah.

We were loaded with Army Infantry and support personnel on each flight out of the air base and ferried back empty for another load. We did that for several days, along with other air carriers who were feeding Savannah from other outlying bases. Somewhere in that period, we had a flight to Oakland, and I had a couple of days off. I also picked up my Left Seat Authorization, which I earned by passing an optional and very long open-book test over several weeks. I was now allowed to fly the aircraft from the left seat at the discretion of the captain. This happened on a regular basis; the pilots of ONA were very generous in this regard, although it was a test as well. The company's philosophy had always been that copilots are captains in training, and captains were to make routine written reports on copilots' progress with this in mind. The downside to this if one looked at the rest of the airlines was that ONA wanted no permanent copilots. The Flight Engineers were not pilots, but all were A&P rated.

Six weeks later with the missile crisis over and two weeks before Christmas, I was furloughed again. I had to laugh when a few of us were reading this second notice in the crew room. A hand-painted sign said, "When the going gets tough, the tough get furloughed." This seemed to be my destiny, but the temptation was to think this might be the last furlough I would have to put up with.

The Executive Terminal and my old offices looked somewhat diminished with a different logo and names in place. I walked through the main part of the building and discovered a new business "Flight Safety, Inc." I went in to introduce myself and see if there were any uses for my current skills. The manager, "Dick Lane," was alone and quite amicable. I told him what I had been doing and what I needed was a job that would let me leave the airlines. He said, "I do not think for one minute that you will not go back when called, George." "It shows that much," I said. He smiled and said, "I will hire you if you will promise me that you will not leave me in a lurch. I would like as much notice as you can give me." I told him I would do that, and we had a deal. He said, "It is not quite a deal yet. I am having breakfast tomorrow with Al who is coming in from New York. I would like you to join us because this is a new branch office, and I want him to pass on you."

At breakfast, I met this famous man. He was Juan Tripp's personal pilot. Juan Tripp was CEO of Pan Am, and Al Ueltschi was a senior Pan Am pilot who was assigned the flying of a B-23, a Douglas "Dragon" of which only 38 were manufactured near the end of the war. During all of this, Al Ueltschi founded "Flight Safety, Inc."

Breakfast went well with very little said about me except for a brief overview by Dick Lane and a very upfront answer by Mr. Ueltschi who said, "If Dick wants you, that is good enough for me." I started working for Flight Safety right away. The first thing I wanted to know all about was the Dehmel Duplicator. I had never heard of such a thing, yet Flight Safety was contracted with several major airlines to do the required instrument check/training for pilots that had previously been done in a Link Trainer.

When I studied the interior, I was delighted to find the instruments that gave me difficulty in transitioning to the DC-7, the RMI instrument and the BMEP pressure instrument. I selfishly decided not only to run this machine properly to instruct in it, but to also spend hours in it on my time off using the DC-7 Technique Manual. I not only did that by flying and reading the maneuvers and actually calling out the power settings that I would be relaying to the engineer and flying the profile required. I did this drill almost every night.

When ONA recalled me, I was set up for a check ride in the link trainer, a much more primitive trainer than the one I had been operating for Flight Safety. The owner and operator of the link sold time in it to the various airlines around the Oakland Airport. He tried to get my job at Flight Safety while I was there and failed, and we both recognized each other. I did not care. I could fly the hell out of it. In fact I got so bored I decided to do a procedure turn for an ILS approach by establishing the bank with the artificial horizon and timing my ninety-two seventy turns without looking at the localizer until I rolled out. When I rolled out, I was right on course but still on the outbound heading. Oh, I had forgotten that in all the link trainers, you have to hold the rudder in or the trainer will not turn. The Dehmel Duplicator flew more like the real airplane and this negative training nuance was a mess. The owner opened the hood and said get out. "Here's your form, goodbye." The form simply stated that I tried to fly down the ILS backwards. No grade issued.

I had to give Captain Starkloff the form, so I dropped it on his desk while he was on the phone and turned to leave, but he interrupted his call to tell me to get back in here. He could hardly talk from laughing. "Flavell, I have no idea what the hell you did, but someday you will have to tell me. The truth is this was scheduled before I was aware of it. You really need your aircraft evaluation; you schedule your link and do everything frontward." Looking at his desk, he pulled a schedule out and said, "We have an airplane at 0700 tomorrow; let's get this done, and just a tip, you should really look at your DC-7 Technique Manual before we go flying." I said, "Thanks but I read that all the time." "I bet you do," said Starkloff. Little did he know.

The day was clear and cloudless. I was already in the airplane since I had done a walk-around before boarding. Starky came aboard with Lesley Forden who was in charge of keeping all of the ONA manuals up to date. He mentioned that Les was also a private pilot and that if everything went well today he would let Les do a little flying. He turned to me as I was already in the right seat and asked me if I would prefer flying from the left, saying, "I know you have left seat authority so it is your choice." I preferred the left seat since I had been allowed to fly left seat by all of the line pilots when it was my leg to fly.

After taking off from Oakland, I was directed to fly over the SFO VOR, a navigation point, and from there to offshore Half Moon Bay. Starky suggested a visual course to the Farallon Islands. My thoughts strayed briefly to the last time I saw them, from the fantail of a troop ship. At this point, a hood-type device blocking my outside visual reference was placed on the glare shield and the check ride began. It was not boring. When it began with the first maneuver in the DC-7 Technique Manual, my pulse raced. I called for the power settings without hesitation, banked into the first steep turn, and for the next hour I was reliving everything I had rehearsed in the "Flight Safety Dehmel Duplicator." After the first half dozen maneuvers were finished, Starky had not mentioned anything or advised me of anything, and I looked over toward him to see what he was doing. He was pointing out a fishing fleet to the flight engineer and Les Forden. I asked him what was next. He said, "What would you like to do?" I said, "The Canyon Approach and Missed Approach." He said, "OK, do it." This is the most difficult thing that you might ever be expected to do with a transport category aircraft. It consists of assuming you are making an instrument approach into a blind canyon that you cannot escape from very easily if you do not have the visibility to land. It requires all the airline pilot's skills in planning, timing, aircraft configuring, coordinating, etc. and at the same time taking the aircraft to maximum capabilities of performance. The escape is demonstrated by performing a semi-acrobatic chandelle reversal. This maneuver is not required anymore, but in the fifties and early sixties, it was still required.

After finishing, I was satisfied, but I would have liked to do it again. I would not get the chance, and it was the last one I ever did in a large aircraft. Starkey abruptly turned to Les and said, "George is going to climb out of his seat, and it is your time to fly the DC-7." Les, smiling and happy, patted me on the back saying, "Captain (which I wasn't) that was a great performance (that was to be determined). This is the greatest event in my life." He was so excited. I was happy for him.

Starky said, "You see those rocky islands down there; you know what they are, don't you?" Les said, "I saw them earlier when you directed George to fly toward them." Starky turned to me and told me that Les had written a book, *The Glory Gamblers* about the "Dole Pineapple Race to Hawaii." Many planes and pilots were lost in that endeavor to win a purse and the glory of having done it. The purpose was to open up the Pacific Ocean, somewhat like Lindbergh had done for the Atlantic Ocean. All had navigated over these Farallon Islands on departing San Francisco.

Back in Oakland in Starky's office, I waited while he gave me my schedule for the next few days. He still had not said a word about my performance, but of course, I had passed or I would not have a schedule. Finally, I asked, "I guess I passed, Starky?" "Oh yes, you did fine; in fact if I knew how well you could do beforehand, I would have had the FAA there to give you a Type Rating." This was great news; now they know I can do it. I began visiting the manuals department after that to say hello to Les. He was such an interesting person to talk to, and his joy of having flown the DC-7 is something that I could share with him. Different levels same joy.

My next assignment was a Frankfurt, Germany trip. The crew would be augmented with a third pilot and a second flight engineer so that no one pilot or engineer would be on flight deck duty for more than 12 hours. I was pre-positioned to Niagara Falls where I would join the inbound crew from JFK. Knowing that they would have to file an outbound flight plan, I proceeded to file the necessary flight plan from Niagara Falls to Gander Newfoundland and gathered all the current and forecasted weather so that the technical stop here would be short.

Tommy Ahearn was the captain. Steedman Hinckley was the international first officer, and I was the copilot, now third in command with a heavy crew. There would be two engineers and a navigator already onboard. Having a heavy crew would allow us to extend our flight deck duty time to eighteen hours. We must be going to be extended somewhere on this trip and probably the captain knew. Anyhow, I am ready and as they come rapidly in, I notice that Steedman sits down and starts flight planning for our route to Gander. I quickly tell Captain Ahearn that not only have I planned it but I also have already filed it and that I do not want to get in any hot water with Steedman. Tommy looks at me then turns back and shouts, "Hey Sted, roll up all those charts and stuff. George here has already filed us." "I know." Steedman is still looking at me, the guy who could not fly the RMI compass system. He looks at me then back at Tommy and suggests that he had better check it. Tommy tells him he already looked at it. "Let us not waste anymore time," and he headed out the door to the crew limo. Steedman walked over to me and asked if I had the latest weather. I told him I had the last weather, but we should probably check on special weather changes. He agreed but we found none.

After climbing out of Niagara and reaching top of climb, Tommy climbed out of the captain's seat and motioned me into it. I strapped in, checked our present position, and set my navigation radios accordingly.

Steedman looked over and smiling said that I did a good job getting the flight filed and putting the weather together. I acknowledged his recognition. He asked me several technical questions that I answered correctly and then he asked me if I had any questions about this flight or anything else. I smiled and said, "Steedman, I have been under the impression that once I got to fly in this seat that I would not have to listen to a bunch of challenging questions from the right seat." He looked over at me with a friendly look and said, "You are right and your answers were also right and I apologize." In the next few days of flying together, I learned that Steedman was a good guy; he strived for professionalism and standardization. In conversing, I discovered that he was only two years older than myself and had been a DC-6 instructor and check airman in the air force. The more I thought of his aviation background the more I realized that we were tracking the same goals and he was two years older; maybe I am on schedule. Maybe I am not doing too badly after all. I had heard that some senior pilots did not like the idea of him instructing or checking them and immediately saw him affected by the same problem that I originally had at Golden Gate Airways. The trip operated to Gander, Shannon, Frankfurt and back to Shannon, Ireland where we went into crew-rest.

That night I met some other crew members from a different flight, and we journeyed into Limerick for a spot of Irish whiskey. Ending up at "Durty Nellie's," we soon switched to soup and Irish beer; later we skipped the soup. Much later when Durty Nellie's had closed, we waited for a bus out at the street to take us to the hostel. Suddenly a big Bentley roared past, then hitting his brakes, backed up to where we were standing. A very heavy Irish brogue spoke, "Err ye lads yanks?" We agreed we were, and the Irish voice said, "I knew it, who else would be standing here waiting for a bus that will not come until tomorrow? Are ye staying at the hostel; if you are, I can give ye a ride." We accepted and offered to buy him a drink at a pub of his choice. Once there we debated his evaluation of the drink called "Irish Mist," which he assured us was a fraud. He said the only good thing in it was a Bush mill Irish whiskey; the rest was molasses and other stuff that ruined the whiskey. After one round and getting the bill, we quickly agreed it was terrible. Terribly expensive that is, and we got on our way.

Leaving Shannon two days later, we continued to be a heavy crew because we were going to Miami via Gander and New York. Before leaving, I visited the "duty free" in Shannon and had purchased a bottle of Chivas Regal Scotch that I now had to stuff deep in my B4-type luggage so it would not break. After clearing customs in New York, we were finally on the last leg, Miami.

Checking in at a rather medium motel that the company representative said was the best he could get, I decided that I deserved a taste of my normally high-priced scotch. I called the engineer, but he was too tired. I tried a couple of the stews, and they had gone out. I had a rule about drinking alone that I have never broken. I only drink with someone or by myself. Adhering to that rule, I broke the seal and sipped scotch of the caliber and price that I usually never order. A couple of those, and I was ready for the sack. Sometime later, I awakened to sounds of passion occasionally rising to "High C." There were voices that I could not make out and although I never thought of myself as a voyeur, I was, after all, a captive audience. That is my story, and I am sticking to it.

If I have to hear the music, I might just as well pay attention to the words. To do this properly, I got up and flattened myself against the wall. Instantly I knew this was going to be the best part of the play. Loud knocks, on the other room's door, followed by a male voice that said, "I know you are in there." A female voice that was so close it sounded like it was on my shoulder whispered, "Oh my God, it is my husband." I pressed even harder to the wall. A man's voice said, "We better open the door." The female voice said, "NO." This is better than watching TV. I hear the sound of the door breaking and then a female scream, "He has a gun." That does it for me. No voyeur here, I hit the floor and elbow-and-knee walked to the foot of my bed. I would have run outside, but voices now sound like they are all outside, and since I am only in my skivvies, I do not want to be confused with the other guy.

The next evening, I casually asked the other crew members if they heard any noise last night, and none did. The engineer said he was dead tired. I said, "Yes I was somewhat like that myself." Before I checked out, I went to the other side of the motel; the door was damaged. Whew, it was not the scotch.

Finally, back in Oakland with a few days off, I visited Dick Lane and talked aviation with him. He was a pilot of yesteryear and still liked to hear current events. I described my check ride on the DC-7 to Dick and let him know how much value the Dehmel Duplicator had been for me. We parted with me telling him that I heard signs of another furlough soon, and he said, "Stay in touch; anything is possible."

Back in Oakland now, I am getting ready for a flight to Tachikawa, Japan. This is almost a replay of my troop ship experience except we went direct. The DC-7 will go via Honolulu and Wake Island. We will also slip crews at each point for rest. Honolulu is always enjoyable on layover; just walking along Kalakaua Avenue or going to Waikiki Beach is pleasant.

Leaving the gate at Oakland, we taxied out through a Tully fog, coming from the northern reaches of San Francisco Bay. It was thick in patches and barely above the ground. We were a ferry flight to Travis AFB to operate the MAC Flight to Tachikawa, AFB. The visibility was all right for departure and as we lifted off, I was busy talking with ATC for an Instrument approach to Travis. Bill Whitesell, the engineer, tapped me on the shoulder and said, "Look out and see if it is feathered." I turn to my window, look aft and said, "Three is feathered; when did you do that?" They laughed. I had noticed a little commotion between the pilot and engineer, but neither one brought me into the problem until they needed to see that it was feathered. Whitesell had picked up the problem on the CRT analyzer and noted that the number 18 cylinder was dead. The captain commanded it shut down and feathered. Many of the DC-7 Abnormal and Emergency checklist items were accomplished between the captain and the flight engineer. We returned to Oakland.

Three hours later, we were in the air again with a different aircraft and proceeding to Travis AFB where we finally originated the flight and proceeded to Honolulu.

The next day en route to Wake Island, I was studying the NDB approach for the airport and had already selected the frequency even though we were only halfway there and still had about a thousand miles to go. There was no reason not to; there were several minutes between required tasks. In addition, each pilot and engineer would always be looking at various gauges in an almost subconscious way looking for a change in indication—a pressure, a temperature, a difference, or difference between engines, something that can be seen by the suspicious mind that would give us an advantage in time or action that might prevent catastrophe. In the Pacific Ocean, the distances between airports seem to make even smooth running engines sound a little rough. We would have a layover there of about 24 hours before picking up the next flight proceeding to Tachikawa. These poor troops being transported will have about 24 hours of flying with only the fuel and supply stops to break the monotony. That still beats 11 days on a troop ship, I am thinking.

About an hour out of Wake Island, the captain made a P.A. to the cabin with our estimated time of arrival and gave them

Wake Island local time along with the news that it was a day later now, since we had crossed the International Date Line.

About 30 minutes out of Wake, I got intermittent static on my ADF receiver. I tried to tune it better, but it was still too weak. I waited knowing that soon I should get a clear Morse code of (dot-dash-dash) (dot-dash) (dash-dot-dash) WAK. It took about three more minutes before I could receive and identify the signal and then I selected the switch to Automatic Direction Finder and watched the needle swing around to almost on the nose. The navigator had been watching me because his navigation responsibilities ended when the pilots were in range of destination land-based Nav facilities. I asked the captain if he wanted it on his side, and he nodded, and now two needles were pointing at the beacon. The navigator made mention of the fact that he brought us 2275 miles safely to this point and now that he was finished, he put his leg up on the navigator desk. I turned to the engineer and told him to make a note of the time, as the navigator was not paid beyond this point. The navigator growled loudly and the ceremony was over. At the higher altitudes, the scattered cumulus clouds were disconcerting in that the shadow they cast on the ocean seemed very similar to an island. The tower had told us that there was no other traffic and we were cleared for a visual approach. There was no airport radar available, but we had weather radar on the aircraft that was used for ground mapping by tilting the antenna down a little until it picked up the island, which we did and found it at the 10-mile range mark. We were at 3000 ft.; our airspeed was slowed now to 120 knots. The Descent, In-range, and Approach checklists were all complete. The landing gear was down with "three green" and the Landing checklist would be complete with full flaps. A quick mental calculation, five minutes to touch down and five minutes to lose 3000 feet would require a rate of descent of 600 feet per minute. None of this would be flown that exact way, but it was enough to know it was well within normal approach parameters for both the airplane and the pilots. One bit of paramount importance was an accurate altimeter setting for the airport so that we were looking at altitude above sea level. At 500 feet, the captain called for full flaps, which I select, check and announce, "Landing check complete." The touchdown brought cheers from the cabin as the troops were ready to get off and stretch their legs, and so were we.

The outbound crew was in operations, and our captain was discussing things with the outbound captain. Our flight engineer was discussing flight engineer stuff with the outbound flight engineer and I found myself talking to the outbound copilot who asked who the "Stews" were on our flight. Shortly thereafter Bill Whitesell came over to me and said, "Guess what, we two are staying here indefinitely until we hear from the company." The Twix that was sent said that we would have 24-hour notice before our next flight. With that news, we headed for the Quonset hut, changed into bathing suits and grabbed some bicycles to go to the lagoon. I had heard there was a Jap Zero on the bottom somewhere but I never found it. The meals were okay, but 4 p.m. was better—the club opened and drinks were 35 cents and beer was cheaper.

Wake Island is so barren and stark as to be fascinating. Pan Am maintained the facility for commercial airlines, for refueling or emergencies. Sleeping quarters are open-air Quonset Huts, and I have never heard rain and lightning any harder or more violent than on Wake Island. Possibly, because of the metal roof and open-air screens set at about a 45 degree off vertical for ventilation and avoiding the rain coming in. The closest other island is Guam, 1500 miles away. The coastline is coral reef attached to the rim of an old volcano, and the deep lagoon is where the crater was. The sea is dark blue and mid-ocean deep except for this anomaly of land. The entire island is about eight feet above sea level with the exception of the airport runway that is approximately 20 feet. Without any wind, there are no waves just a chop where the reef begins. A tsunami would not be a pleasant thought.

The next day more of the same until about 3 p.m. when an ONA flight came in for refueling and servicing en route to Tachikawa. Pan Am sent a jeep to get us out of the lagoon. We were told to get ready that we were leaving. We got suited up and met the captain at operations. We told him we were expecting the 24-hour notice, but he interrupted saying, "Makes no difference; you are in crew-rest right now. We have six bunks onboard, and it is your turn to sleep. You will join your previous captain in Tachikawa and immediately return to Wake Island while my crew goes in the bunks. The company is multi-crewing all military contracts from now on, so the only limitation is 120 hours flight time in 30 days and 24 hours free of all duty once each seven-day period and of course 1000 hours a year. There is a bulletin out that we should get in Honolulu explaining all of this, so the bottom line, gentlemen, is we two crews are going to operate straight through from Wake island to Tachikawa, Wake Island, Honolulu, Los Angeles, then to Waco, Texas."

Well it all went the way it was described except the bunks left a lot to be desired. The top bunk would have been easier to get into if you could have started out in a horizontal position and just slid into it. There was hardly any headroom to maneuver but we made do. It was somewhat pleasant to lie there in the bunk and know that you were on full flight pay. Since sleeping is one thing I do well, it amused me to think I was finally being paid to do this. The more I dwelled on that thought, the more I expanded on it. Right now, I might be the highest paid person in the country being paid to sleep. No, the captain would be making more. Well at least I am a professional sleeper in training. My English teacher in high school would have expected as much. I was starting to jiggle the bunks, laughing until another crew member complained saying, "I hope you're reading something funny up there and not playing with yourself." I assured him that I was playing with myself.

CHAPTER 7

Scramble to Survive

Back in Oakland, the word was furlough. I heard it even before I made it to my mail folder.

I went back to Flight Safety and talked to Dick Lane again. He asked if I was through with ONA, but he did not have anything full-time and nothing on the Dehmel Duplicator because the person I trained was doing fine.

Dick said he had a U.S. Forrest Service Instrument Ground School coming up that I could teach if I had a ground instructor certificate. Well I already had that, so the job was mine when they come into town. In the meantime, I could brush up on Federal Aviation Regulations as affects Corporate Flying and in a week make a presentation to Kern County Land Company. He said, "Also there is an individual with an Aero Commander 680 that wanted to get his Instrument Rating, but I have to have you on the payroll for insurance requirements. If you are willing to do all those things, I might just as well. Can you give me two weeks notice when you're recalled the next time?" I assured him of no less.

I was hired to prepare for that group, and in the meantime, I requested three excellent 16-millimeter films titled *Sub Sonic*, *Trans-Sonic*, and *Super Sonic*. I planned on any excuse to show customers these films because I had never seen anything as good for explaining Jet Flight, and Jets were coming quickly to Corporate America. Standard Oil, based at San Francisco, had a Sabreliner and a British Viscount.

One of Flight Safety's customers, "Kern County Land Company," was familiar to me but only because I knew a copilot who once flew for them on their DC-3. I envied him thinking this is a job for life, but he eventually left to go to work for Western Airlines.

Jim Gray, Chief Pilot of Kern County Land Company, and his copilot, Luis Poire, showed up for their annual FSI review, and we got down to business. I did not know much about their company, and they were happy to give me some information. KCL was number five in profits vs. gross in Fortune 500 the previous year. They owned 40% of the Mooney Oil Fields in Australia. They had oil wells in Canada and the Gulf of Mexico and owned 8% of the county of Kern in Bakersfield, California, the 8% being an oil field. "Well that explains the land and the oil," I said, and they said no. The land was a different asset. They owned 2.8 million acres of land in the Southwest Four Corners area. They owned 40,000 head of cattle feedlot in Minatare, Nebraska, and another 60,000 head of cattle in a feedlot at Bakersfield, California.

In fact, they were getting a new Piper Aztec shortly to be based in Bakersfield. Currently they flew a Convair 240, which was based in the Pacific Southwest Airlines Hangar at San Francisco. I mentioned that I was surprised that PSA had enough room leftover to allow a private aircraft space with offices included. He replied that the hangar was built and paid for by KCL to have space for their corporate aircraft, and there was some sort of lease purchase for PSA.

The next week was busy for me because all the senior managers of the US Forest Service from each district in the United States were coming for a ground school on Instrument flying. Some were pilots; some were not, but all did a lot of small airplane flying. Fire patrol was a big item in each district. They were an interesting bunch, and even among themselves, they did not often have the chance to interface like this. I made it a rule that they could interrupt at any time to talk, and I would continue when they were ready. They were not going to become instrument pilots in one week, but they would learn what they would need to do to survive. After that, they would have to have airplane time and an instructor anyhow. They loved it, and I think they left knowing the hazard of getting into instrument conditions without the training and without the aircraft being properly equipped.

One of the managers offered me a job saying, "I cannot offer it to you because it is civil service, but if you take the test, there are selections made on what the service requires and some latitude exists there. You would have a cabin, a canoe, a rifle, a jeep and an aircraft mechanic that would live about a hundred yards away. The aircraft would be a Dehaviland Beaver. Your food and education for children would be covered, and you would fly fire patrol and other flying as needed by the service. I used to fly a Cessna 180 on Edo-Amphibian Floats out of China Basin, San Francisco, and so I am not without some experience. I will always wonder about that dream.

About this time, I thought I would call Captain Starkloff with ONA and let him know that I would appreciate any information on a possible call up of pilots since I really needed to give Flight Safety a reasonable notice. He said that anything he would say would not be firm, but he thought if I gave 30 days notice now, I would be very close to what they seemed to be planning. I gave this information to Dick Lane, and he suggested I interview some applicants and he would hire another instructor on the Dehmel Duplicator. He wanted this to be someone with a Ground Instructor rating and then he would have more flexibility. I thought this was great and everything went as planned. Just after I had mentioned that he was ready, I went home and found a Registered Letter from ONA. Hot dog, this is my recall. Wrong, I was terminated. I was stunned. I sat down to read this again. It said that they were closing the Oakland Base and everything would be moved to Idlewild Airport, New York. It continued

75

by saying that I did not have my probationary period of a year in yet, and that I would be terminated in accordance with the terms of the ALPA contract that states that during the one-year period a pilot can be terminated without cause or recourse.

At first, I thought I had a year in, but of course, the furlough time did not count. I called the New York office saying that I would make my own way there, thinking that they did not want to pay for a move and all the collateral expenses of that aspect. They were not interested. If the day I saw the sign that said *Learn to Fly* was the biggest turning point in my life, than this day is the next biggest turning point. I was not happy about this turning point, but who knows.

Just because you want something very badly does not mean you will eventually get it, yet it seems just as paradoxical that others get what you want without seemingly trying and without any apparent appreciation. My seniority was lost; my rights to recall were nonexistent; my record showing I was ready for a type rating in the DC-7 was now irrelevant.

This was the lowest point in my airline life. Just becoming an airline pilot was not enough; the tough part was remaining one. Had I gotten the type rating, I would have felt justified in wasting all that time. However, coming away with nothing but the experience, well that counted, so I needed to quit whining.

I did not want to go back to Flight Safety, even if I could. They have been a big help, but I was there to keep my goal intact, not to stay on the ground. Besides, I needed to find a flying job period. I thought of KCL; Jim Gray had said they were getting a new Piper Aztec. Jim Gray—time is everything; I call him quickly and explain my situation. He was interested and accepted my application but warned me that downtown had the final say. Moreover, he said, "Are you sure you will move to Bakersfield because the move has to be soon if you get this position?" I told Jim I would do everything it took to have this job.

It was a small six-place twin-engine Piper Aztec. It will be fully equipped from the factory for IFR Flying; this is not what I wanted to do, but I would consider myself very lucky to have a job with KCL, a company with plenty of money, with a Chief Pilot that appears to be a good boss. Quit whining. I was still at Flight Safety for a few more days to round off a week at Dick Lane's suggestion. He had been a good friend. The phone rang, and I heard the FSI secretary say, "Yes Jim, he is right here." "George, it is Jim from Kern County." Hot dog, I rush to the phone. I answer and Jim said, "I am afraid that someone else has gotten the Aztec job." I quickly said, "Jim, I am really disappointed, but I know I had a fair shot at it, and I want to thank you for accepting my application." Jim responded with, "Don't you want to know who took the job?" I did not really care but I said, "Who?" Jim said, "Luis Poire, my copilot." "Oh well then do you need a copilot?" "Yes I do and if you're interested, I would like you to come over to the hangar and fill out another application." "I am on my way, sir."

CHAPTER 8

Corporate Pilot

Things were looking much brighter. I got the job. Jim was great to fly with. My ONA experience dovetailed well with what he did and expected. The airplane, a Convair 240 with Pratt & Whitney CB-16s, was a real performer, wet power and all. There was seating for about 14 passengers if it was ever filled up. The plush seats in back were on tracks that allowed four of those seats to swivel and belly up to four around a table. Two couches behind the cockpit were made into wide berths with separate curtains. A large bar area in the very back of the plane was well stocked and it was one of my duties to keep stocked. The only meals we served were Delta First Class, and all of our catering equipment was bought from Delta so they had no problem with loading it for us. We had to be careful though that they did not substitute our equipment because ours was not all beat-up. I was an important customer where I bought my liqueur since I bought one or two cases a month. I did not dare tell them I was a pilot; they may never fly again.

Kern County Land Company is an old-line company that went back into the early 1800s and only went public in the early part of the 1900s. It was cash rich and made investments that way without stock transfers, etc. They had financed a couple of guys named Bill Hewlett and his partner Dave Packard when they were getting started in Palo Alto.

The year before I started with KCL, they were number five in *Fortune 500* magazine in profit vs. gross income. They were a cash rich company. They also owned 40% of the "Mooney Oil Fields" in Australia, oil wells in Canada, oil wells in the Gulf of Mexico, and their heritage, most of the oil wells in Bakersfield, California. People asked why it was called a Land Company then. Well they own 2.8 million acres in the four corners area of the U.S. They plant 100,000 acres in the Southern San Joaquin Valley with 12,000 acres planted to experimental crops. They have a 40,000 head of cattle in a feedlot in Minatare, Nebraska, and a 60,000 head of cattle in a feedlot in Bakersfield, California. They also invest in manufacturing; they own Walker Manufacturing in Racine, Wisconsin. Walker is a manufacturer of automobile parts and accessories. Not long after, I was employed they bought J.I. Case Tractor Company for 60 million cash. The president of the company and CEO is also a member of the Board of Directors of Lockheed Aircraft Company.

Having been around airline operations, I guess this sort of corporate operation, including a connection with Lockheed really impressed me with the wealth and employment security that I felt. Jim had been an airline pilot earlier in his career so he understood what I had been trying to do. He also had a highly qualified friend that wanted this job but had recommended me because there was ten years between our ages, which was better from the company's standpoint.

Three months after I started, Jim decided we should have more than one captain and provided training at Flight Safety for me in New York. They had a Convair simulator that had recently been installed and were happy to use it. Completing that course, I passed the check ride with the FAA in Oakland using the company Convair. There were two KCL mechanics at the hangar, Bill Johnson and Charlie Bradley, who was also a pilot. Charlie was now used in both capacities as needed.

Now I had a type rating, the Convair 240/340/440, actually three type ratings one could say, since it applied to each of them. Now I am making progress, but still not four engines, as ONA was so insistent about. This was 1963; some airlines were still using Convairs, and I was type rated. I had made more progress in four months than I would have ever dreamed possible.

Over time, I had heard of good and bad corporate jobs. My job was not good; it was excellent. We usually had a schedule that went a week or two in advance or more. We were never on-call or stand-by and always had reservations at the best hotels where possible. The only exception to that was a trip to King Salmon, Alaska, with the Chairman of the Board as the only passenger. He had warned me days ahead of time that our accommodations would be less than extravagant but that might not be any better because he would get off the Convair and climb in a Super Cub that would fly him on to Naknek, Alaska, where he would visit a cannery and remain overnight. Well our room was on the second floor, and the wooden stairs leading up to it had steps that were worn down in the middle from foot traffic. The first room I came to belonged to us and, uh, oh yes, about six other men. One man was sitting on his bunk, saw me and said, "If you're just getting here, there is two over there." "Thanks," I said, "my copilot is on his way too." "Your pilots," he said. "Most of the rest are too." The trip back was great, and we left with enough salmon and king crab to start a restaurant.

I saved the king crab, but I gave the salmon to a friend who owned a restaurant in Palo Alto, Sam Jones; he called the place "Sam's." Sam was a gentleman of the old West, soft spoken and tough as nails. I met him when he was the head chef at "Tarantinos Restaurant" on the wharf at San Francisco. I was giving flying lessons to Don Lynam, one of the owners. When Don was not there, Sam would come out to see who was asking and then he would tell the bar to comp me. He was second in charge, and between them, I could eat there or drink there on the house. I tried not to abuse that privilege but probably not too hard.

Don would often come down to Harpers for his flight lesson, bringing a dozen shelled clean king crab claws ready to eat. He would tell me he had Sam clean them up for me. Ah the influence of the flight instructor when they first discover the sky god. The truth was that for all the years I knew Don he was always the same. They opened up a new additional restaurant in Sausalito called the "Spinnaker" in about 1964, and the first night open was a private affair including the Governor, the Mayor of San Francisco and all kinds of dignitaries, except for me. The San Francisco Fire Department had fireboats spraying water on the roof of the building, and the best part was everything was free.

A couple of days later, I stopped in to see Sam on the way to the airport. I was now living in Fremont, California, in a brand new four-bedroom house I bought on the GI Bill for $19,950. I would leave the house early about 7 a.m. and drive over the Dumbarton Bridge straight to Sam's. It was hard to pass up a quick hot cup of coffee when I was going to the hangar for a non-flying day anyhow, so I would make a left turn almost directly into the driveway of his place. Usually it was too early for the front door to be unlocked, so I would go around back and tap on the window, and he would let me in. As I stood drinking free coffee, I asked how the fish had been. He looked at me frustrated and said terrible. I was stunned; I asked what was wrong. He said, "Everybody is talking about what great salmon that was and want to know when I am having it again, so naturally I start checking suppliers and even Seattle does not have that size and quality in any quantity. When are you going again?" I tell him that I think this might have been a one time thing, sorry. He tried to talk me into joining him in the businesses, which he is serious about, and I am not.

I applied myself to be an expert on the Convair as far as specifications, performance and weight and balance, just anything that was in the aircraft manual. I also studied the engines. The R-2800 cu. in. was America's first 18 cylinder radial, the double wasp. A new way of making the cooling fins had to be employed. They had to be machined from the solid metal of the head forging. All the fins were cut together. A gang of milling saws was automatically guided as it fed across the head so that the bottom of the groves rose and fell to make the roots of the fins follow the contour of the head. The engine had no competition as it started out with 2000 hp and evolved to 2400 hp and finally 2800 hp with 115-octane fuel and water injection. KCL had the CB-16 engine but without the carburetor modification that would be necessary for CB-17 power; we used 100/130 octane and water on takeoff if required. The Convair had been used to Racine, Wisconsin, a number of times. The eastbound leg was comfortable, mostly because we left San Francisco at the end of a working day where relaxation and dinner soon followed. With restful chairs and/or beds for the executives, a good night's sleep was possible before arriving in Racine early in the morning.

The opposite occurred on the westbound leg because they usually finished their business by 3 or 4 p.m., and the flight home was longer due to the prevailing winds so that they would arrive at their homes very late in the evening.

Some thinking, about a possible Jet Aircraft, was beginning to surface. I remember having the Executive Vice President onboard for one of these long westbound flights. I had gone into the cabin to stretch my legs, check how everyone was doing, and of course get some coffee. The Executive Vice President asked me how much one of these new business jets cost. "This is really something for Jim to answer; he is very much checking all of the possible selections in detail." The cost was the last consideration after performance and economy of operation. Anyhow, I come up with some ballpark figure of about 5 million dollars, and this old boy's eyes squint up for a minute and he said, "Well, we just drilled the deepest damn hole we have ever drilled up in Canada around the Peace River, and instead of oil, we hit a solid vein of pure copper that is not recoverable and came up dry. That cost 5 million dollars. I think the next time we think of that we should buy a jet. I am going to tell 'The big C.'" Dwight Cochran was the CEO; Jim Gray was a detail person, and to a great extent, so am I. In my case I think it comes of laziness; I prefer to think a procedure through and do it that way every time, or to study something in great detail so that I will not be surprised by something I had not considered. Jim had been going through all of the possible jet aircraft that he might present to the company at some point if asked. He had settled pretty much on a French Aircraft with the unlikely name of Mystere 20 and had gotten company permission to go to France and gather more information.

Somewhere in this timeframe with the company's close relationship with Lockheed, Jim and I had a chance to go through a stationary mock-up of Lockheed's proposed Super Sonic Transport (SST). Boeing had built a similar one. These steps were part of a government dictated design-off, this as opposed to a fly-off, which of course would be millions of dollars more. The mock-up had a five- or six-seat section of the cabin, and the cockpit had a working display of the retractable nose that showed the sub-sonic and super-sonic positions as seen from the cockpit. The cockpit and cabin were full scale, which created the major questions. The cockpit surprised crews with its small size, and the cabin surprised people with the small round windows. One question regarding windows was: what happens if a window blows out? There were two answers for that also: the pressurization would remain the same, and do not go near the window. The other question was: why are they so small? This had two answers also; the small size gave it more strength and hopefully prevented you from going out the window.

Not long after seeing the mock-up, I had the pleasure of meeting "Kelly" Johnson. He along with the President of Lockheed and some others and the President of my company were onboard. We were going to Burbank from San Francisco. Once we were at our cruising altitude, Mr. Cochran rang the interphone and asked if Mr. Johnson could visit the cockpit. I acknowledged that, and soon Kelly was sitting in the jumpseat saying that he was relieved to be away from all the high-powered people in the back. I told him that he was the high-powered person onboard as far as I was concerned and that I was pleased he came into the cockpit. He thanked me and noted the good visibility of the Convair. With that, I mentioned the SST mock-up that I had visited and asked him about the difference of the Boeing version and what he thought of it. He described his "Double Delta" wing design that was excellent in cruise and yet worked fine at low speeds. He said the inboard "Delta" re-invigorated the air on the wing during approach and landing, producing low stall speeds, whereas the Boeing design accomplished this by swinging the wing, straight for slow speed stalls and swept for High Mach Speeds. He finished by saying that the swing wing was no good. I smiled at him and said, "You're just saying that because you did not use it." He said, "Young man, I hold the patent on it." He continued, "Any time you can change the shape of the bird before or during flight, the results will be optimal for all realms of flight. The reason it is no good, at least for now, is the weight. All the monkey motion to make it do these things is too heavy and anything less is too weak. The metallurgy as well as the presses in this country has to be improved to do it right."

Later in the year the real oddity that came out of the FAA's decision to award the contract to Boeing was the modification of Boeing's design. They scrapped the swing wing and redesigned the wing along the lines of the double delta.

Somewhere in this period, I had asked the question of "why would we not consider the Lockheed JetStar?" since Cochran was on the Board of Directors of Lockheed. Jim dismissed this with data that appeared to make that aircraft unnecessarily expensive. It was not long after that a decision was presented to the aviation department. We would be getting a Lockheed JetStar, albeit a used one. NASA had one that it was returning to Lockheed and "Kelly Johnson" of the "Skunk Works" would be getting our Convair.

The aircraft was delivered to the aviation company that would be installing a new interior and exterior paint job conforming to the KCL standard. This aircraft would then become N104KC. Jim Gray and I went to the Lockheed Plant in Marietta, Georgia, for ground school. If I thought the DC-7 ground school was difficult, this one was an electrical nightmare. The instructor for that subject was very good and I learned many terms that would help me with future jets. The difficulty I was having was the electrical schematic. The generators were also used as engine starters, one of the last large civil aircraft to start that way. Pneumatic starting was the future. The electrical power to start was provided by two large nickel cad batteries, wired in "Series," for the first two engine starts. The next two starts would be with the batteries in "Parallel," done automatically through a Start Series Relay Switch. The difficulty was in answering questions using the electrical schematic that were on a large pull down roll that was mounted on the ceiling with other subject schematics. My salvation finally arrived with a pilot instructor who started the class one morning before the written exams. He walked in and said, "I am going to tell you gentlemen a few things that will help you today. The most important subject is this," and he walked under these mounted schematics with a wooden stick and hooked the "Electrical System" and pulled it down. My heart sank. I was dead meat. He said, "This schematic that I am sure you are all familiar with by now is as important as a 'Bowl of Dung.'" He smartly released it, and I watched it roll back into the ceiling. Reaching up again, he pulled down an overhead cockpit display of several switches. "Here is all you have available to control everything in that schematic. Either individually or in combination, these switches will accomplish everything you need to deal with." At the end of the day I passed.

Kelly Johnson had designed it to be a two-engine jet for the Air Force, but when he found out that the Air Force would not buy the British Bristol Orpheus engines, he had to go with four American Pratt & Whitney engines. Other than the complexity of the electrical system, it was very straightforward. In fact, if you notice, it has de-icing boots and is the only aircraft that I have ever flown that is certified for flight in "Maximum Continuous Icing Conditions." Only once did I have to use that system, a very long time ago in a hold at Chicago. Another thing that I found interesting was the way it handled in turbulence. It "shuddered" is the only thing that comes to mind. The more I think about this jet, other than the fact it was my first jet, the more I remember of so many new things it introduced. The Doppler Navigation System for instance which we studied in great detail only to find that the "Memory" flag was almost always displayed if you were counting on it, like on the ocean. "Memory" is telling us that it has not dumped the information it had, but it is deaf, dumb and blind about where it is now. I was particularly suspicious of the Land/Sea switch that was supposed to enhance its reliability, depending on the surface return. If I selected "Sea" when actually flying over water, it would wait about 30 seconds before slipping the "Memory" flag into view, so I just assumed it was the manufacturer's way of avoiding any liability if we got lost.

The Depleted Uranium episode was a little more obscure. Charlie Bradley, our mechanic/pilot who was a prince of a human being and fountain of knowledge about radial engines and rebuilding them, and I were going to do a studied walk around the JetStar. We would take turns on who started, describing each item or section of the plane and proceed accordingly. Somewhere around the ailerons or the elevators, I have forgotten, Charlie raised his voice and said, "Don't touch that." I said, "This?" and touched it again. We went through this a couple of more times, as I played with the notion that I was pressing a button that made him talk. I finally said, "Why not?" He said, "Because." I explained that I might not be the brightest bulb in the pilot fraternity but try to ratchet up the explanation a little. He said, "That is depleted Uranium." "OK," I said, "but what part of 'depleted' do I not understand?" Well he was as much at a loss as I was, and said so. Nevertheless, he was right; it was in the manual. As for the term depleted, I know when a beer bottle is depleted; maybe a Geiger counter is not the same.

The Pitch Trim, now this is a beauty. The entire empennage moves; in fact, it moves so far as to take the elevators out of the range of any authority and makes the aircraft look a little strange. Why would they do this? Probably the stable stall or deep stall that plagued many manufacturers and test pilots when installing rear-mounted engines. These aircraft would get in a stable nose-up position that was out of elevator authority and no amount of yoke travel would change anything. Some test pilots died because of this. The JetStar, with its moving empennage I think, would allow you to run the trim to a down position and recover.

When landing, the use of normal trim would leave the tail looking odd when taxiing to the ramp, so many operators, including KCL, were placing the empennage in a more normal looking aircraft position that happened to be out of the range of elevator authority. A flight that I ferried out of Monroe, Louisiana, provided an experience that I still remember. The checklist which called for setting the trim was in progress during taxi-out and was interrupted for a clearance read back while setting it. When the checklist resumed, it was picked up, starting with the next item. At rotation, I found myself with the control column in my lap against the stop as if the elevators were not connected to the airplane. Not even a little movement, the nose wheel noise grew even louder. The scrub pine trees were rushing towards us, and there was not room to stop. My thumb went down on the nose up trim, with or without my conscious thought. I held the yoke back against the stop and finally saw the nose moving with the speed of the jackscrew slowly rotating us. I was not yet sure whether we would clear the trees or not. It was going to be close. We broke ground with excess speed because of the slow rotation, and I translated that speed into an excessively steep climb that just narrowly missed those treetops. That was as close to disaster as I would ever be. It was pure and simple pilot error, and we both knew it. Had that trim reached the proper point, and we then flew into that forest, they would have had no clue about what caused the accident. If everyone likes to fly with experienced pilots, there were two of us this day that became more experienced.

The JetStar had a drag-chute, which was required to be checked and repacked on a time schedule, so we deployed it one day, landing at San Francisco. It created a lot of conversation on the tower frequency. It also had an interesting Speed Brake, located slightly aft of the mid fuselage. It extended downward like a barn door and was very effective and quiet in speed decrease and descent management.

Jim Gray came in the office one morning and said, "Kelly Johnson would like someone from the company to come down to Burbank and check out a crew on the Convair. That will require getting them a Type Rating, so one of us will have to go down there. I thought you might like to do it, but it is up to you." I said I would like to do it.

In Burbank after a night's sleep, I arrived at one of the least used gates. Going up to the guardhouse where three guards were working, I started in with the words that were given to me. I showed my driver's license, said my name, and then said my birthday is 10-16-32. "Well," he said, "they must have the cake and ice cream over at the main gate." I said, "No, I am supposed to come through this gate." "Who told you to come here?" he asked. "I do not know who, he didn't tell me." "Well come on in the office here such as it is and we will try to find out." He tried the employment office and did not get anywhere with them. He said, "What is the nature of your business?" I told him, "I was instructed to come to this gate and present myself the way I did, including the numbers I gave you."

"Wait a minute," said the sergeant to the others, "This could be Skunk." He dialed a couple of numbers and then turned to me and said, "They are sending a limo over." "I think it is coming now," said another guard. The car did a turn and beeped its horn. No limo though. I went over and shook hands with one of the Lockheed pilots who took me over to where he parked his limo/car, and we walked the rest of the way. He did not know what I was there for, and I did not tell him. I asked to see the Chief Pilot, and he walked me to a corner of a large hangar and pointed to his office. I went over and introduced myself, and he was expecting me. I was introduced to some other people I presumed were pilots, and then the two that I would be working with. We spent the next half hour in the office with the Chief Pilot talking a little about my background and how much time I had in the Convair, which was not all that much since corporate flying does not use the aircraft like the airlines. I talked about Golden Gate and ONA and flying the DC-7 which they liked to hear since they were flying Super Constellations with the same engines as the DC-7. The Chief Pilot did not have much to say except that time was of the essence. He did not look happy and asked how long it would take to get them "Typed." I said, "A week from Friday." "Really," he said. "How do you figure that?" These guys here know what they are doing if they fly those "Connie's," and if I can have the airplane for the ground school with an APU attached for power, we will live and breathe in the best classroom you can get. That will take three days and then two days flight training and two days doing the flight test. A week from tomorrow we will be done. You will have to schedule the FAA for Wednesday of next week.

"You are sure you can do this that quick?" asked the chief. "I would rather you estimate longer and make it than to have to tell my boss that it is not going to be on time. He is a man that likes us to do what we say we can do."

"We will still have Sunday off and get it done." "Ok," he said. "What time will you start tomorrow?" I turned to include the pilots and said, "Eight o'clock, bring a lunch. We'll eat on the airplane and go home at four o'clock, if that is okay with everyone." "One thing," said the chief, "I want you to promise me if there is any doubt for any reason that this timetable cannot be met you will let me know as quickly as you can. And one other thing, if you have a problem of any kind, like maybe the APU or Fuel Service, any problem, do not try to work it out, call me right away." "Okay, will do," I said.

The pilots and I walked towards the flight line and one turned to me saying, "You know who he reports to, right?" I guessed, "Kelly Johnson." He smiled and said, "Be quick, be quiet and be on time. That is our boss." About that time I saw lines of men in work clothes with lunch buckets, boarding one of the Lockheed Super Constellations. Engines #3 and #4 were already running. "What is that all about?" I inquired. He said, "Rule Two." Oh, okay. As we approached the Convair, an Auxiliary Power Unit was being towed up to it. I lowered the rear stairs, and we went up into the cabin. "Hey, real plush ground school here," said one. "Nice bar here," said the other. "Do we have a Happy Hour?" "Absolutely, it starts at 4 p.m. and that coincides with our leaving." Aw rats.

At the end of the day, the Chief Pilot stopped by with some information for his pilots and a gate pass for me. I opened the envelope, and it was a plain piece of red plastic without writing or anything else. I thought it was strange, but the next morning it worked fine. That night I received a different colored one in exchange, and so it went the entire time I was there.

The training was going well; the flying went smoothly, as I had expected, and when Wednesday came, I met with the FAA agent and he and I went out to the airplane and sat in the cabin. I went over my qualifications to be teaching in a large aircraft, and then went into the FAA approved flight manual page by page, indicating what they had been studying and what I had tested them on. I suggested that the manual was his to peruse for the oral exam and the flight exam for purposes of correct answers and/or actions. I explained in detail the maneuvers that I would put them through, which entailed simulated engine failures at different critical points of flight and all other maneuvers that I determined met the requirements of the regulations, and then asked if he felt successful performance of those as described were sufficient as he understood them. He indicated that should be all right. My reason for being so outspoken to the agent was that the General Aviation office did not do that many Type Ratings for large aircraft. That was usually the forte of the FAA Air Carrier District Offices. I felt it was necessary to make sure that we were all on the same page before we began.

To the credit of these fine pilots, they performed well in all aspects of the examination, and the FAA agent was complimentary in signing their paperwork. A few weeks later, I received this original letter sent to Jim Gray from "Kelly Johnson" of Skunk Works Fame. I unfortunately did not take very good care of it, and it ended up buried in the attic.

LOCKHEED AIRCRAFT CORPORATION
BURBANK, CALIFORNIA

29 December 1965

Mr. Jim Grey
Chief Pilot
Kern County Land Company
600 California St.
San Francisco 8, California

Dear Mr. Grey:

Our pilots asked me to write you a letter to tell you
what a great job Mr. George Flavell did in checking
them out on the Convair that we purchased from your
company.

Under Mr. Flavell's able supervision, the pilots were
able to assimilate a maximum amount of training in a
minimum period of time. He was dedicated to performing his duty in the best possible manner, showed a high
degree of knowledge and professional skill, and was a
credit to the pilot fraternity. His training prepared
two of our Lockheed pilots for their FAA type ratings,
which were secured without a hitch. The pilots feel
extremely fortunate to have had such able, capable supervision during their training on the Convair.

Thank you very much for furnishing such a high caliber
man.

Sincerely,

Clarence L. Johnson
Vice President
Advanced Development Projects

CLJ:vmp

Letter to my Chief Pilot, Jim Gray, by "Kelly" Johnson

(He had addressed it to Jim Grey.)

92

Photo of Lockheed JetStar given to KCL showing exact aircraft from NASA lease and prior to our complete renovation of interior and company paint job with Wagon Pin Logo. (circa 1965)

Back from the training in Burbank and en route to the hangar at San Francisco, I decided to stop at "Sam's Place." I tapped on the window, and Sam's smile lit up and invited me in. He started right in about me joining him in the business. "I have no children; it's going to go begging when I am gone. I will teach you everything." "Sam, you have already taught me everything I would need; like everybody steals, it is just a matter of time." "Make money on everything even the cigarette machine. Do not get a manager; he will go in business for himself. Overpay the help; they will stay longer, but fire them when they steal. Do all the buying of meat, wine and liquor yourself. Keep an extra supply of prime meat and know it when you see it because the driver will try to give you choice, and I would have to tell him to put it back on the truck. Tell the driver he will not be coming back if he tries that again." "Good, very good," said Sam. "Now learn this, you see that hole in the window over this side of the kitchen? That is from a rock thrown through it last night. I called the sheriff and told him and they will be ready. You see it is a test to see what happens and no alarm goes off. Tonight or tomorrow night, they will break in through a window here; they will head right to the bar, and that is what will set off the alarm. Those two small two-foot long swinging doors which they could just duck under are wired at the hinges and the signal goes to the sheriff, and he calls me to come down and sign the charges when they catch them." "Wow, I am impressed but what if he or they have guns?" "Will not matter. The deputies put one Doberman in the back door and one Doberman in the front door and the thief or thieves will be standing on the bar screaming, 'Call off the dogs.' You know I guess these guys do not talk to other thieves in jail because this has happened three times since I have been here. They could steal hundreds of dollars of meat or wine from the basement, but they cannot seem to resist walking into the bar." My coffee was gone, and having heard an interesting story, I went off to the airport.

The next day, I had a trip to Ontario, California, a short hop from San Francisco.

The big "C" had a board meeting at Lockheed Burbank and then a Lockheed "Missile Firing" to observe before he came back, so it would be a long day. Mr. Cochran thanked us for a nice trip and mentioned that he would try to give us an hour's notice of his return. We had parked away from the terminal since a limo was waiting his arrival out on the ramp to ease the transition to the meeting. Parked now at an angle to the blast fence, I was sitting in the back of the aircraft eating my "Delta" First Class Filet Steak and Eggs, reading the boss's *Wall Street Journal* and thinking how great this job had been. It had been well over three years now. In the background, I heard a jet starting its takeoff. The noise of acceleration was very loud and getting louder; this was no Boeing 727. This sounded like a DC-8. What a great jet that is and they were building an even newer stretched version. I was waiting for it to clear the blast fence and quickly it rose just next to me; the noise was incredible. I saw the cockpit come into view as it rotated and I was thinking what a sight. Then a stunning blow. On the side of the fuselage, it says *Overseas National Airways*. I was dumbfounded. Like an old lover that never got over it, I was hurting. This dream had walked into my life again, and I was not handling it well. I had seen an ad in the paper about six months ago saying that ONA was hiring DC-7 copilots in Oakland, and I did not even investigate. I was no longer a copilot, and besides I was already flying captain on a four-engine jet. I was making more money by far than a DC-7 copilot was. I could always call if I wanted to just be curious, but what if they made me a tempting offer? I might make a bad decision; it would be better if I did not tempt fate.

I waited almost a week before I made a decision. It was risky but so is everything worth doing. Jim had been the biggest help, but the last raise he requested for me was rejected because my rate of pay progression was too fast.

I stopped at Sam's to have coffee. I told Sam that I had to make a long distance call and would pay him for it. I called ONA in New York and asked for Steedman; he was enough on the inside track to be able to tell me what was going on and the chances of upgrading to captain and the pay. "Mr. Hinckley's office, can I help you?" "Yes, Captain Hinckley please." "Mr. Hinckley has someone in his office right now; may I tell him who is waiting?" "Umm, this sounds awfully formal." I waited and Sted answered the phone. "George, how are you? What are you doing?" I told him that I was flying a JetStar for a corporation here in San Francisco. "Ah the bay area, I wish I was still living out there. I miss the Alameda Hotel. What can I do for you?" I said, "Well if anybody would know what was going on back there, you might, and I wanted to consider coming back if it would be worth my while." Sted brought up the JetStar saying that it was a four-engine jet, correct? I agreed, "It is, and your flying captain on that." I said yes. He asked me to hold if I could, that he wanted to find something out before he could confirm anything. I waited, thinking he was probably well connected, if he could confirm anything! It took awhile but he finally came back. "George, we have six DC-9s that will be here in 60 days; you could hold a captain's slot if you can come right back within a week or so." I asked him what that paid, and he asked me what I was earning with KCL, and I bumped it $200 a month and gave him that figure. He hesitated, but then said, "OK if it is a deal right now?" "Wow," I said, "you have some authority to do this over the phone? What is your title these days?" He laughed and said, "You don't know?" I said, "No I don't know." He said, "Well I am the President and CEO." "Chez Sted, are you kidding me?" "Do we have a deal?" he asked. "Yes we do." "OK, when you have made your travel plans and have an ETA, call Jack Hogan and give him the information, any questions?" "No sir." "Glad to have you aboard, George, see you when you get here." "See ya." "OK."

CHAPTER 9

Return to Non-Sked

It was time to exhale now. I thought to myself, by God, I may not make good decisions, but I sure make big decisions. The obvious questions I could ask myself would be: are you crazy, is this not the airline that kept laying you off, by the way didn't they fire you, etc. The funny thing was I was happy. The next funniest thing was having Steedman hire me; wasn't he the guy that doubted your flying skills? Maybe I must be masochistic; life is too boring knowing where my next meal is coming from. It did not take long for the worry to start because as soon as I checked in at JFK, I heard that we were not getting the DC-9s. I went to see Steedman, and he indicated that the problem lay with Pratt & Whitney, the engine manufacturer, as they were on strike. Douglas Aircraft was parking production line product awaiting engines. Well I was on minimum flight-pay guarantee; that was not bad, but furlough would be the logical move if I were management. Fortunately, Steedman wanted me to fly a Rockwell Jet Commander that one of the Board of Directors owned. I would have to go to school for about a month and get a type rating. I readily agreed and that took care of any immediate concern, and besides Steedman had already given me back a seniority number that would have been mine, as though I had never been terminated. I had not lost everything as I had supposed.

I finished the ground school and returned to JFK. I was introduced to Chuck Glaze, a new ONA pilot that was flying it presently and who had been a JetStar pilot as well. We became friends. He started to teach me to fly the Jet

Commander, but we were unable to continue because he was of the school that memorized everything and had a set power setting for every conceivable configuration. I gave up and told him to read the checklist. Before it was over, I told him to just be a safety pilot, checking for other traffic that I would instruct myself, which I did and passed a type rating ride with John Dosster in Allentown, Pennsylvania. Chuck and I remained good friends for years after.

I had moved to Cherry Hill, New Jersey, when I was informed that I would do all of the flying on the Jet Commander. The aircraft was based in White Plains, New York. At first there was not too much flying, but then it was chartered out to the Penn Central Railroad during its merger with the New York Central Railroad. I presumed Steedman had some influence in that to justify my hiring. The end result of this assignment was that I had to drive from Cherry Hill to White Plains, New York, to pick up the CEO and executives to fly to Philadelphia Airport, and then return them to White Plains later in the day and then drive home. This had just barely begun when I received a letter from Johnson & Johnson Company looking for a JetStar Captain. I responded to that, and then asked ONA for a 90-day leave of absence. I thought correctly that getting me off the payroll for a short time would be acceptable and it was. This also gave me protection and a good option for permanent employment if things looked shaky with ONA. The flying with J&J was very good; the aircraft was kept in spotless condition. I could understand why they wanted an experienced JetStar pilot since the plane was based in Linden, New Jersey. The runway was rather short and had obstacles on either end. The Chief Pilot had told me that they hardly ever have anyone onboard with a title less than president. I asked how many presidents it took to run the company, and he told me they have 77 vice presidents of J&J who are presidents of other owned companies. They had two other aircraft including a beautiful DC-3 whose use went back several years. It had about 15 seats, panoramic windows, and a cockpit where the bulkhead had been moved back several feet, allowing for a navigator station. He even had a large "Globe" which hopefully was not needed for a last resort. The chief pilot said that many of the executives prefer it when going to Washington. It was very comfortable, and it would get there at about the same time as the JetStar and can use the short runway there, which they usually were assigned. The other aircraft was a Convair 580 Turbo-prop. A few weeks later, he told me I was going to Washington, and we better go shoot some landings for proficiency. I said, "What are you talking about?" He said, "The DC-3 and I want to see you fly it first." "I cannot fly the DC-3. I do not have a type rating." "What?" he shouted, "On your resume you had DC-3 experience." "Yes I do with Allegheny Airlines and Aloha Airlines, but I do not have a type rating." He found my resume and confirmed what I said. He said, "Come on, let's see how much work you need to get typed." When we came back, he said, "I am going to get the pilot that flies it a lot, and he will give you the necessary instruction to go get the type rating." The following week I went to Allentown, Pennsylvania, and got my type rating from the FAA District Office Manager, John Dosster.

I was assigned the next DC-3 trip, which was to Boston in some rotten weather. Maybe it was only bad at the lower non-jet altitudes, I was thinking. Even with Allegheny Airlines, I had not seen it this bad. We were de-icing the wing about every five minutes, and the windshield was frozen over, but we had the heater hoses for that when landing. Alcohol on the props but the side windows solid ice. It seemed we flew for hours, but I guessed I was spoiled from the JetStar. Finally, Boston was in sight near the bottom of the ILS. This was a trip back to yesteryear. The weather was not the biggest thing; it was the antiquated technology that I had not thought about for years. I do not even remember the trip back, so I guess either the weather improved or I was now very proficient with the past.

The strike was over in a few weeks, and the engines were being shipped to Douglas, and I knew that soon there might be pressure on my leave of absence. All is fair in love and employment, and since I was on 90-day probation, I felt my job ethics were fair. Just within a few days of the leave, ONA called and said that I had to be in Long Beach, California, for DC-9 Ground School on the following Monday. A couple of days later, the chief pilot of J&J gave me a performance review which was passing but nothing to rave about and which if I had any thought of staying disappeared at that point. I thanked him for the review and reminded him that a 90-day probation worked two ways and that I enjoyed everyone that I worked with, which was very true, but that I would be leaving now and wished him the best.

Reporting for ground school in Long Beach, California, I met an old friend, Jim Fink, but found myself meeting several pilots that I had not known before. They were the ones hired since the closing of the Oakland base a few years earlier. They knew me though, at least by name, because I had been placed ahead of them on the seniority list, and they were not happy about it. I apologized for my good fortune, and since they informed me that a grievance had been filed with ALPA, I suggested that they abide by whatever comes of that since I would have to do the same. With that, I made friends. At the end of the ground school and with all tests completed, we got a weekend at home.

Reporting to New York for tickets, I checked my mailbox and among many other things found a new seniority list. I was listed at the very bottom. A note attached to it said that I would still be paid for my status as Jet Commander pilot, that I would be trained and checked as a DC-9 Captain, but not paid at that status until utilized.

We all returned to Long Beach for our flight training. Jerry McCabe was my instructor, and he told me that the chief pilot on the DC-9 had instructed him to teach me in the right seat, but that for the check ride if I seemed ready I was allowed to take the left seat for a type rating ride at the instructor's discretion. I think the best comparison is for a layman to drive an English stick-shift car vs. a U.S. car.

What a mess management and unions can make of things, but I always felt having a union for pilots is the best alternative so I did not care except to get on with it. In the end, I passed my type rating ride.

After a few weeks back in New York, I thought that status had changed quickly since the company wanted a DC-9 ferried to Atlanta where Eastern Airlines was going to provide a maintenance check on it. Al Wintermeyer was assigned as copilot. Al was not type rated on the DC-9 yet, but he was senior to me. As we flew south, he thought about this and mentioned that he thought he should be paid bypass pay since he was entitled by seniority to receive the equivalent captain's pay. I agreed with him. Well we had two days to wait so we hung out together. Going to lunch one day, we had to step aside in the hotel parking lot to let this guy in a brand new Cadillac El Dorado back out. He swung around as we were walking on and rolled down the window. "Say fellows, I have a deal for you if you're interested. I am a large watchmaker sales representative, and last night I had a great time with this little lady I met and spent all my cash money. I really need a little for things you cannot really write a check for. I have a watch here," pulling one of dozens like it from the back seat. "This is the latest thing," and handed it to me. I opened the case, which felt like it must cost more than the watch and looked at it. It said "Electric" on the face and the smooth running secondhand looked like solid gold. He said that these were giveaways to the big jewelry stores that were his customers, but he had to sacrifice them today for $50. "You would be amazed at what they will sell for in the store." I turned to Al, "You have $50?" "Ah, yeah." I bought it. During the lunch, we took turns looking at it in the case and finally Al said, "I think you got a deal." "Yeah well, you have to take the cookie when the tray comes by." Later up in my room, I hated to take it out of the case because it looked so good in there, but I finally did. I wondered about the stem and what function it had if it was electric. Hmm, I pulled it out; it felt rather cheap. I started to wind it, and the noise was like a windup toy. Hmm, I called Al and told him I felt bad getting this good deal when it was his money buying it. I told him I would turn the watch over to him if he wanted it. He said, "What's the matter with the watch?" "It is a cheap piece of junk although I think the case might be worth something." He was laughing so hard I started to also. Later in the week, he was telling someone as I walked up and said, "George, show us the watch." I said, "Gee I would like to, but I sold it to Chuck Glaze." Al said, "You dirty rat; what did you charge him?" I said, "$75," and he said, "You didn't." I said, "You remember what the guy said about the store price and all that." He didn't talk to me for a couple of weeks until he found out I had given it to Chuck with the provision that he give me $10.00 if it keeps working. Well, Chuck either kept it handy to put on when I was around or the thing ran for a couple of years. When I asked about the $10, he said he couldn't be sure that it would keep working. Al took his pay claim to the company later, and they paid us both copilots' pay because the contract said that captains' pay starts with the first revenue flight and since this was a ferry flight, it was not revenue.

Eventually we were all trained; I had my type rating early, but the bottom line was that nothing had really changed at all. Everyone had to have 100 hours as copilot before being a captain in the specific aircraft, and by the time it all shook out, we were all flying captain anyhow.

I flew several Las Vegas charters, many St. Martin trips, and a few CAM flights for the military, but eventually I bid to fly cargo on the "LogAir" military contract that ONA had been awarded. The reason for this was that it was a scheduled operation and somewhat more stable as it pertains to home

DC-9-32CF ON THE LOGAIR CONTRACT (circa 1967)
The contract called for a maximum cargo uplift of 34,000 lbs.

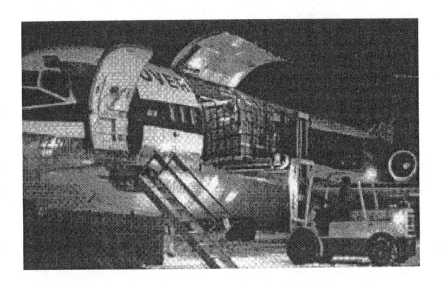

There were four Standby Rocket Engines, two in each Wing Root that were armed at Hill AFB to provide power on demand for Second Segment Climb in the event of engine failure.

life. This operation was based initially at "Wright Patterson AFB," then another was added at "Warner Robbins AFB," and then with the addition of a Navy "Quick Trans" contract, another one at "Alameda NAS." ONA was the first airline to place "Turbo Jet" aircraft on "LogAir," and I was the first line pilot to fly a trip, having received the aircraft from two of our management pilots "Lou Furlong" and "Phil Brown" at Warner Robbins AFB in 1967.

During the three years that I flew the DC-9, ONA pioneered many new improvements for achieving maximum payloads. The first was a new chart, The Zero Flap Takeoff + 12%, which allowed us to carry 34,000 lb. payload out of Hill AFB. It was an FAA-approved Extrapolation of Douglas Performance material. I asked the question of what does the 12% stand for. I was told it was roughly a 12% increase in speed, which gave us roughly a 12% increase in payload. I suggested a 12% increase in pay, but it fell on deaf ears.

The next was to use "Standby Rocket Power," two in each wing root to assist what is known as "2nd segment climb." The ability to meet the proscribed rate of climb with one engine failed. Since this chart is built upon the engine failing at V-1, the speed at which you can continue to accelerate and take off or stop. I suggested to the company they should perhaps point the rockets in the other direction, but like that comedian, I get no respect. What the heck, I was now a rocket pilot but without a pay increase.

It did cause a few problems because we were operating next to the maximum tire speeds of about 225 mph. We lost a couple of tires that shed rubber, not air, but then found out this was only with retreads and not new tires. There were other side effects caused by the re-treaded tires. Landing at Tinker AFB at Oklahoma City, we touched down in one of those super smooth landings that occur only when you are not trying. A scattered shower had lubricated the runway and absolutely removed any feeling of arrival. In my peripheral vision, I could see the copilot's head swing in my direction just daring me to brag about the landing. Instead I remained stoic, looking straight ahead, leaving him to comment. After talking to ground control and getting a clearance to the terminal, he turned back and said, "You know, making a smooth landing like that with water on the runway can cause rubber reversion which hurts the tire." I said, "I know, and I was trying to bang it on harder but I have not mastered the technique that you have." "Are you insinuating…" "Yes," I said. He replied, "Man, the first liar doesn't stand a chance." The copilot had gone inside to work on the departure paperwork, and I was idly chatting with our company mechanic. Finally as the sun was getting higher, the mechanic said, "Well I better do a walk-around, and then I am going home, see ya."

A loud holler came from the mechanic standing by the left landing gear, "Look at this Captain. What kind of landing did you have?" The tire was holding normal air pressure, but only little triangle pieces of tire were visible at the wheel hub; everything else looked like canvas The mechanic said that he was going for a spare wheel and would be right back and that maybe we could get out on time. That rubber came off on takeoff was what I believed and maybe the flap had some marks to prove it, and as I looked at the flaps, it dawned on me. We had made a zero flap takeoff, and the rubber would have gone in the engine. I quickly shouted at the mechanic and told him to forget the wheel and to get a ladder. He argued, but I insisted. When he returned, I told him to look in the left engine. "Wow," he exclaimed, "take a look at this." It would involve an engine change. Had we used any flap extension, the path of debris, tire pieces included, would have been physically deflected from engine ingestion. Thus, the cost of zero flap extension and retread tires held another operational and financial consideration.

LogAir carried many security items, and the chain of custody was of particular concern when anything "Secret" was carried. All of the ONA pilots flying on this contract had "Secret" level clearances.

The first occasion of "Secret" material that I carried started on a sour note. The paperwork was given to me after it was loaded in the aircraft, and worse, it was on the first pallet loaded, which put it in the rear of the aircraft. I said, "Before I sign for it, I am supposed to see the items, identify the labeling as 'Secret,' and sign for it."

"I know, Cap, but here's how it works. You're signing here without seeing it; the foreman at McChord will sign for it sight unseen because otherwise we have to unload eight pallets here, and if you insist on this request, they will unload your aircraft last at McChord because you will be late." I took note of the fact that my copilot had listened to all this and decided to go on to McChord.

Arriving at McChord AFB, the "K" loader came up to the cargo door and the ground crew was shouting to open it up. I declined and spoke to the foreman about the secret material and asked him to sign for it. "I do not do that until it comes off the airplane, and I see it," he said. "I was told you would sign off for it sight unseen." "No way, what I do is sign it much later after all the flights are in and put the copies in operations for the pilots to pick up the next day on their outbound flight." "Well that is not the way it is supposed to work." "Well it's been working that way for sometime." "So you're telling me that you're signing for them after you see the item itself?" "Yes sir, that is what I am saying." "Well you can see the dilemma the pilot is in; we go into crew rest here, leave 'Secret' material in the hands of someone else without a change of custody." "I cannot help it if you cannot stay here until we get to it." "Well here is how I am going to fix it. I am going to call the base commander and advise him of our situation, which you say is not new and has been going on for sometime, and tell him that I want an armed guard put on the aircraft until I am rested enough to return to the airport and make arrangements for the transition of custody." He winced and said, "Give me that paper. I will sign it before you screw everything up."

A few days later, there was a notice on the bulletin boards of all the Air Freight Terminals stating that classified materials will not be placed in the aircraft prior to the pilot in command signing for it. Well half the problem was solved, and I would resolve the arrival problem later.

Dover, Delaware, presented a problem when we started operating in there as part of the LogAir program. I had been in there previously without a problem since I had what is called a 180/181 form. It is a combination of legal talk that basically states that the company will not hold the military responsible for any accidents and that we will be responsible for any damage that we do to the airport. These Hold Harmless forms had been around for years and were always carried in holders mounted on the inside of the cockpit doors.

This particular time, I was just getting on the aircraft when a sergeant approached me and said that he could not find the 180/181 papers in the cockpit door. I suggested he follow me, and I would look for them and we both made a search of that area and another possible location without success. I asked him if the LogAir Contract Form would suffice since that was in the holder where the other forms had been located. He said no and mentioned that he did not want to cause a problem but that he had other aircraft he had been assigned to refuel. I said, "Sergeant, I was an airman second class earlier in my life, and I respect your effort to try and help. I want you to disconnect and go about your duties and if anyone questions why you left this aircraft you tell them it was at my request, okay?" "Yes sir, thank you."

I went into the Air Force Operations office and told the sergeant there I wanted to send a message to Wright Patterson AFB. He handed me a form, and I filled it out. *Attn: Commanding Officer: LogAir, due to non-acceptance of LogAir Contract which is now carried in the aircraft in lieu of 180/181 forms, fuel is not available. Crew is contacting company for hotel or further instructions.* The sergeant read that and said, "Woe, wait a minute. I can get you fuel." I asked him if it was his job to get our aircraft refueled. He said, "No but I know someone over at the fuel farm." I told him, "Please stay out of a work around solution because I do not want to go through this every time I come here." He said, "Ok, if this is what you want." "It is what I want, Sergeant."

I went out in the open walkway that led to the ramp, bought a Popsicle from a machine, and waited. It was not long before a major in a blue car skidded to a stop on the ramp and walked quickly toward operations. He looked at me, but I suspect he preferred not to talk to anyone eating a Popsicle and banged his way into operations before turning around and asking me if I was off the aircraft out there, pointing as he talked. I said that I was, and he said, "What is the problem?" I said, "I do not really know except that the motel limo was supposed to be here by now." I thought his neck was going to explode. "I am talking about refueling your aircraft." Oh that, "Sorry that cannot be done; you see, the man that refuels the airplane has no authority to do that without the 180/181 forms." "Yes he does, that is he will." "What I mean is that there is a truck coming now to fuel your aircraft and the sergeant inside said he tried to help you and you would not accept his help." "That is absolutely correct, Major. I would rather correct this problem at the source and not have to hear from a refueler an apology for not being able to deliver fuel, or have the sergeant in operations offer to get someone he knows to solve the problem, and I was not waiting for a limo. I was waiting for you or someone like you to fix it." Now flipping my Popsicle stick into the trashcan. "If you do not have the authority to fix it permanently, let it be known that the message I sent will go out every time I or another ONA pilot comes through here and is told that they cannot refuel. Our airline is judged by the Air Force and in particular "Wright Patterson" as to our on-time performance, and this type of snafu is detrimental to me and my company." He looked and spoke to me with a different tone and assured me that this was already resolved.

I said, "Thank you, Major," and extended my hand; we shook and departed. I did not tell him I was an Airman Second Class. I never had that problem with Dover AFB again.

In spite of checklists and individual safe-flying habits, things happen. A crew in Warner Robins walked out to their aircraft that they had just flown in earlier and was now reloaded for departure. The copilot extended his walk to include a walk-around of the aircraft, climbed the stairs, and then retracted them into fuselage and locked the handle. The stairs would not be a problem, but an unauthorized person had closed the cargo door. Someone who was not a pilot or a mechanic but a company manager of ground services who was deadheading on the flight and wanted to be helpful. It flew open and upward right after takeoff. The interior molding and soundproofing was peeled off the door and ingested into the Number #1 engine. The captain, Bob Francis, did a commendable bit of flying to return safely to Warner Robbins. Since the door light did not illuminate until after the incident, there was no indication in the cockpit to warn them of an unsatisfactory latching. It became an immediate Airworthiness Directive (AD) by the FAA and a fix was implemented including a need for one of the pilots to physically inspect the latching mechanism of the door from inside prior to entering the cockpit.

The DC-9 had an inherent problem that occurred with water on the runway during takeoff and landing. The nose-wheels would spew a fire hose-sized water stream directly into the aft fuselage mounted engines on their respective side. It was so accurate they might as well have designed it that way. The fix for that was to design a nose-wheel tire with a "Chine" on the outside wall near the tread that would deflect the water enough to eliminate the problem. In later years, a flat plate-like spray deflector was attached, eliminating the special tire. I mention this history as a prelude to the following story.

The ONA LogAir aircraft in addition to the center folding jumpseat was there primarily for FAA Inspectors to observe any flight at their discretion or for company check pilots when doing line checks or other observations. It also had a bench-like seat that was located behind the copilot and could seat two people. This was to accommodate military couriers and others with military passes to ride or check our compliance as well as to check the loading and unloading done by the civilian contractors at the airfreight terminals.

On this particular night, we had three pass riders, one of whom was an Army "Bird Colonel" who wanted the center jump seat and got it. He was not a pilot and was worried about the possible weather. He was right to be worried about the weather, but I was more worried about the possible vomit.

We would be leaving Nellis AFB near Las Vegas, Nevada, and going to Hill AFB in Utah. The weather at Hill was at minimums and forecasted to stay that way. I was fueled to go to Hill and hold for one hour and then return to Nellis if necessary. That equates to full tanks. We took off and were doing fine until we got to Salt Lake City when I found that they had gone below minimums and had traffic holding at the Salt Lake VOR. At the same time, we received the same information about Hill AFB, which is only a few miles further north. Salt Lake Center put us in a holding pattern along with their other traffic knowing that we were really trying to get into Hill. I would gladly accept landing at Salt Lake at this point if they come up first because it would save fuel and time in the process of continuing. We could see the clearing to the west that was being talked about by other aircraft on the center frequency. The colonel decided to query us about so many things that I had to ask him to refrain from questions. I thought I might go to headsets, but I decided it was better for everyone to hear how busy we were and therefore keep the talking down. Hill weather RVR was improving, and the ceiling was estimated at 100 feet. However, we had been holding for an hour. Suddenly Salt Lake was accepting arrivals, and the pressure was somewhat off, but things can change for better or worse. Salt Lake was just holding at minimums so the clearing to the west was not the factor here. We could talk to Hill as much as we wanted; there was no traffic there. I could see the weather improving; we could see the Great Salt Lake better and it was definitely a moving clearing trend. Salt Lake had improved to 300 feet ceiling and two miles, a good sign. We had one and one-half hours of fuel, a clearing trend to the west and an open airport below. We checked the runway conditions at Hill, and we were told that there had been one inch of new snow. We asked for the total depth of snow and whether it was dry or wet snow. The only thing they were reporting was the one inch of new snow without any more information. Suddenly Hill weather was VFR, and Salt Lake was below minimums and the airport was closed. We were vectored out of the holding pattern at Salt Lake and requested an ILS from Hill. I could take it in as a visual from here, but I was thinking I would get a better runway condition report from the radar guys. No luck, same old story, which did not conform to our runway contamination definitions. One hour and fifteen minutes fuel now, which was considerable but not in our location. The RVR suddenly reported minimum levels in blowing snow. Glad now that I requested the vector to the ILS, I intended to land. The colonel decided to tell us that he could not believe how we could navigate in such poor conditions, that he could see nothing. I agreed with him, but silently. I had always made it my judgment call to start the APU when conditions were poor, although the checklist did not call for it. We were on the ILS inside the Outer Marker now, and I did not want any distraction started in this cockpit. I was cursing myself for not doing it earlier. The strobes were in view then the approach lights appeared and then there were runway lights, but I dared not to do anything but fly the ILS They are only points of light submerged in a world of white that defines nothing. I had no slip in place because I had no reference. The aircraft touched down; the spoiler handle clicked but did not move and my hand pulled it up, aft and up again as a natural instinct. This deployed the spoilers manually. It was caused by the sensor that senses weight on the wheels but no spin-up. I could see that we were in a slight crab, but it did not matter because had I done a sideslip on flare, I would still have to crab it now on the surface because there was no friction and we had a crosswind. All the lights had been put on by the copilot on my command as we touched, and now as we rolled out, they seemed to be more of a hindrance reflecting snow, etc. I did not have to worry long; they went out when the nose came down. The engines had flamed out from slush that was too deep for the "Chine Tires" to be effective, and we were hurdling down the runway in a dead airplane. There was no electricity, no hydraulic power, except accumulators. I told Jess Williams, the copilot, to turn emergency power on and start the APU. It did not start; we were still moving pretty fast, and I saw no reason to slow it as there was a high-speed turnoff coming up that looked like I would be able to clear the runway on it if I did not use the brakes. When we finally came to a stop on the turn off, it had all been done without any breaking. There were fire trucks all over the place. Jess said that there was a fireman hollering something to him and pointing to the rear of the airplane. I suggested he open his window and see what he was saying; that he may know something we did not. When he opened the window, I could hear him. He was saying, "The fire is out." Heck, we could have told him that. They towed us into the gate, and we deplaned. The Army Colonel asked me if things like that happen often. I held myself back from saying, "Every time it snows," and assured him truthfully that I never had that happen before. Ah, the experienced pilot.

The tower wanted to talk to me, and once in the Air Freight Terminal, I asked them how they had gotten the fire trucks into position so fast. They said that shortly after they saw our landing lights appear, they went out and two big balls of fire appeared. They punched the big button that was the Crash Alarm. They wondered what caused such big balls of fire, and I explained that what they saw was the fuel in the engines, which was by design always on fire, and was washed completely out of the engine while still burning. We were going into crew rest anyhow, after I made a report to the company and talked with our mechanics. The APU failed to start because during the start cycle a ram air door extends to provide sufficient air; only in this case, it filled with wet snow and then closed. It was cleaned out and cycled properly, and the APU was started. Several things including engine inspections had to be done before the next flight and were done in time for the next crew, Bob Francis and his copilot, flew outbound to Mountain Home AFB, the next morning. Not long after, Overseas National put DC-9-32CFs on the LogAir Contract; the company bought several Lockheed Electra 188s from National Airlines, no relation to ONA. They were converted to straight cargo aircraft and carried a 34,000 payload, the same load that the DC-9 carried. In addition, a unique use for one of the aircraft developed a lucrative sideline, the movement of race horses around the country. ONA for years was the only carrier of the most famous horse of all, Secretariet.

Nearing three years of flying the DC-9 on the LogAir Contract, I had a chance to bid Captain on the DC-8 based in New York. I would be the junior captain, which really does not mean much with a non-sked. The trips are mostly international, and unless you want to layover in Madrid, this week instead of Rome or want to fly with a certain crew there was not much difference. I would fly on Christmas and other holidays and maybe I would have my days off broken into smaller segments where commuting home was more difficult. It was time to transition to this aircraft, and it was important to me. This is four-engine time, my dream. It is also more job security, if furloughed I have another type rating to offer in the non-sked market. It is also an opportunity to fail. Each new aircraft carries that risk. Putting that in the proper prospective, every airline pilot has dozens of chances of failing, whether it is a new airplane or not. No Guts, No Glory. On the other hand, No Pay, No

Porsche. It definitely takes more bourbon to make these decisions. Getting a type rating with a non-sked is an experience in itself, and we are one of the best, if not the best. The ground school was our own, and the Flight Engineers were in the same classes; they were professional A&P Engineers. This is very important because a lot of the knowledge that the FAA likes to check is the nuts and bolts of these airplanes, and in type ratings, we learn more about what we have no control over than at any other time. We have two types of DC-8s and two types of configurations for each. On one side is the DC-8-63 which is the stretch version, the heaviest, the largest, the most powerful and carries the most fuel and passengers and is convertible to a freight configuration. There are weights, volumes, lengths, pressures, limitations, maximums, minimums, load factors, positives, negatives, ratios, flows, temperatures, angles, degrees, positions, selections, red lights, amber lights, green lights, flashing lights, steady lights, indications, horns, bells, clackers, chimes, etc. Many values are different for the smaller DC-8s, and both are different in cargo configuration.

This information readily available for study is two telephone book-sized manuals for each version of the DC-8. The last day of ground school is the written test. I hate written tests; they have to have a failure rate to qualify as legitimate for FAA reasons. In other words if everyone always passes, it is too easy. Well, 70% is passing, and everything else is a waste of brain cells, a carryover from my high school days, but then I think of Steb and try harder. I usually score in the high 80s or low 90s. Nobody is counting except if you fail. The final grade is "Pass" or "Fail." I passed. I do not remember what I had. I do not care.

The next step is an Oral Exam by the FAA, one on one, by appointment only. I am scheduled, and the Chief Pilot said, "You must take your application with recommendation for oral exam signed off, and by the way, take the manuals for both aircraft." I wince, "You're kidding, all four manuals?" "Yes." I drive over to the FSDO office at JFK. I make two trips to carry my briefcase and the four manuals into the office. I do the same thing again when I am invited into the interoffice where the agent sits with a leg on the desk. As I turned to get the other two books, the lady who greeted me has brought them to me; I was grateful and thanked her. The agent motioned me to a seat. I sat respectfully and put my application on his desk, and he looked it over and then pushed it back to me and whispered to me, "Put how much simulator time you have." Since I did not have any simulator time, I did not pick it up. He looked a little annoyed; he used a pencil to point to the area in the form where simulator time would be entered but continued talking on the phone. I ignored him. He finally ended his call saying he had a problem he had to deal with. I would not engage him yet, but he had no idea of the fire he was building. He said, "I am asking you to put how much simulator time you have in the DC-8 Simulator." I paused, and said, "I have no simulator sir." "Well then, you are not qualified to be here for the Oral Examination."

"Let me explain the situation, sir; every month Overseas National mails me a check. In exchange for that, I allow them to tell me what to do from time to time and they have sent me here to take an Oral Examination." "Well I do not feel it is fair to you to be here without the benefit of simulator which would put it more in prospective for you; who is in charge over there?" "Captain Starkloff is Vice President of Operations, sir, and the number is right here on this memo to me."

"Starkloff, this is Warren at FSDO; you have a man over here for an Oral that hasn't even seen a simulator yet. No you're wrong. I will not give the man an Oral because…He hung up on me." "That is all right. I will leave until you have it straightened out." "No I want you to stay here until I talk to my boss." His phone rang and he was only listening and saying, "But, but, I did not think, but, all right, yes sir…My boss said I have to give you an Oral, and I think the only thing we are going to prove here is that you are not knowledgeable enough to pass." If I had doubts before, I sure had no doubts about this guy's ability to make an ass of me. Yet, he had two bosses mad at him already, his and mine. I love to turn defeat into victory. I told him, "I have my marching orders to be here, sir, so fire away." He grabbed one of the DC-8-63 books and started asking questions, and after that, he would ask whether my answer was for the –63 aircraft or the –50. Well I am not the brightest bulb in the building, but he was looking at the –63 manual and so I answered accordingly. Finally, he started changing books and zeros in on some of the most obscure questions that I have ever heard, but I am not comfortable enough to debate. Without telling me during any of the questions whether I am right or not, he said, "Well I think that you can see that you are not ready yet, do you agree?" "No I do not agree for the following reasons. There was not one question that you asked that would have even been addressed in the simulator, and further, I am already a captain on several jet aircraft such as the Lockheed JetStar, Rockwell Jet-Commander and DC-9. If you fail me, I am not going to see the simulator that you think would help so much. I am going to go back to a three-day crash course or something like that and come right back over here again." He slowly leafed through the –63 book, and, then finding what he was looking for, started going through the Limitations Section. This from his or any instructor is known as getting a clean failure. Not knowing a small number of limitations can be used as a gross example to failing someone. "My God, the man does not know the Limitations of the Aircraft." He does not have to explain that he asked the person the maximum number of negative G-forces allowed on the DC-8-50 series, when in the cargo configuration. I knew it. I had studied these thoroughly for the simple reason that I had been told as a student pilot to know these cold. If an examiner is thinking of flunking anyone and wants a good reason, they will resort to "Limitations." When he was finished, he looked up and said, "I am going to give you a chance. It is obvious to me that you have done much study on your own." After he signed off the Oral Section on the application, I waited for him to give it to me, but he started asking if I wanted him to call transportation for me. I declined and pointed to the window and said, "I think I see it coming now," he turned. I picked up the application, thanked him very much, and left.

In Denver, Colorado, now I stood in front of the United Airlines Simulator building and thought about that United personnel manager who thought I would never make it as a pilot. I have pretty well proved him wrong so far. I wondered if he was making it as a personnel manager. Inside, Hugh Monteith, my instructor, greeted me; he was surprised. I was not. I had his name on my instructions for reporting here. Monty, as I knew him, was a Captain with ONA on the DC-7s when I was his copilot. I knew he had gone to United as a Flight Instructor, and it was a real pleasure to find he would have me in the simulator and the aircraft portion of training. I do not remember much about the simulator, but I recall a few details about the flying aspect of it. I remember flying the "White Whale" as they called it, and I enjoyed every minute of it. He asked me one day who gave me my Oral, and I gave it to him and handed him my application, which he needed anyhow, and he asked me how I did. I explained the whole thing to him and he laughed. I had him here with some other FAA guys whose district picked an airline for a flying refresher among other things, and he was the only clunker of the bunch. I could hardly get him sharp enough to reach 500 feet on the ILS and still be lined up sufficiently to be able to land straight in. It figured that those few are the ones that try to make up with authority what they lack in ability.

In 1969, the DC-8-63 was the biggest thing in the air, 187 feet long, wingspan of 148 feet, 26,000 gallons of fuel, and a maximum takeoff weight of 355,000 lbs. The pilots that would be flying these aircraft would be the most senior by pilot seniority lists and generally older since these numbers are generated by date-of-hire.

Being in training here at United Airlines, I am an anomaly. I am 36 and here for a DC-8 type rating because I hold a captain eligible number for this aircraft with my airline. A sort of big fish in a smaller pond. I am not without awareness of this, and there are some that think I might be the youngest captain in the world flying this aircraft. All of this is pure conjecture and particularly so because I have not passed the type rating yet or the other company checkouts that ONA will give me for this particular model of DC-8, or the Company and FAA Line checks that will automatically come along during actual revenue flights.

The DC-8-63CF Largest of the DC-8 Series Aircraft
254 Passengers, 355,000 lbs Takeoff Weight

The DC-10-30CF, The Largest DC-10 Series Aircraft
380 Passengers, 555,000 lbs Takeoff Weight

The day of the Type Rating is now, and I awoke at 3 a.m. without an alarm and lacking confidence. I went through some Emergency Checklists that have Memory Items, and other Abnormal Checklists, as well as Limitations of all kinds. I am fixed on the forest and seeing all of the things I can be asked that I do not know by memory. I have to get a grip. If you do not know something, you know where to find it and never bluff. I told myself, I have done this before, calm down. I dressed in Levi's and a leather jacket and went outside; it was cold. I found myself walking through an industrial park that was busy. Exercise helps; I knew that it wears the body down a little, which helps with the stress. I waved at a few people that just wave and kid about the cold. I wonder what they would think if they knew why I am here. Time was going by.

I am dressed in jacket and tie now and waiting at a table in the United Airlines Training building. I have a mindset to relax and be myself. I reminded myself to just do the best I can, that this is just the first step of experience to come and that others have been here before. My instructor pilot will be flying copilot for me, although we have a different flight engineer who introduced himself. He asked me if I was nervous. I told him a lie; he didn't believe me. My instructor said, "Stay in charge, George, never quit, never give in; there are only two of us in the cockpit that can fly this airplane. The engineer cannot, the FAA cannot, and I am not touching the controls." Therefore, I am all alone. "Okay, you all do what I tell you, and I want you to know that I have a lot of experience looking for a job."

The FAA agent showed up; his name was Oscar Bird. He was the head of the FAA office in Denver and doing this check-ride because all of the other agents were assigned airlines, and ONA was not one of those since it was based out of New York. He said he was the only one left and that is the trouble with being the boss. Turning to me now, he said, "Have a seat and we will get started." The others went to the aircraft.

"Well young man, this is a big day for you. I do not quite understand how someone your age would be in this position, but of course, the major airlines have people in the right seat who are just waiting for vacancies. Tell me your background; the paperwork shows it, but I would like to hear it from you." "Before I tell you, I would like to tell you a story about a friend of mine, not too much older than myself who was a line copilot for United and became a vice-president of maintenance flight test. One day he was sent back to ferry a DC-8 from Chicago to San Francisco because it needed a ferry permit. They would not give him the airplane because he looked too young. It turned out all right, after several phone calls. I think I fall somewhat in the same area. I have flown for Aloha, Allegheny, ONA on the DC-7, captain on the DC-9, and now able to hold the DC-8."

Oscar was very frank in telling me that he would watch carefully but fairly. Once airborne, we headed for Pueblo, Colorado, with a few maneuvers in between. Arriving there, we made some touch and go(s), engine failures simulated by pulling the power levers back and finally a "No Flap" approach, which is done at a much higher speed, since the wing stalling speed is much higher. Oscar did not like this since he felt I was flying it much like a normal approach, whereas it should be a flatter profile. He said he would like me to do another try at it. This approach will not touch down because no airline likes to actually put the aircraft on the ground because of the high tire speeds and possibility of losing tires. I did the approach again, giving a much flatter approach, which I would have done in the real world but was reluctant to do during the test. It is one thing to fail by being too high or too fast but being too low or too slow is a deadly reputation to overcome. I passed and was now rated as a DC-8 pilot. Several months later, I talked to my instructor in Denver, and he asked if I had seen the letter that Oscar had sent to United and which he had forwarded to ONA. I told him, "Maybe, but I do not remember, tell me more." He said that Oscar had written that he did not remember anyone who

121

had flown the DC-8 any better or appeared to have been more at ease in doing it. I had not seen it, but I thanked him. It is difficult to guess how you are doing, and it is probably better not to know anyhow.

I got my DC-8-63CF checkout, and I was on my way back to international flying—including London, Amsterdam, Frankfurt, Paris, Madrid, Malaga, Rome, Athens, Cypress, Palermo, Tangier, Rabat, Casablanca, Marrakech, Fez, Oujda, Zurich, Vienna, Milan, Geneva, Dublin, Budapest, Prestwick, Oslo, Copenhagen, Venice, Cairo, Agadir, Jeddah, Khartoum, Niamey, Kano, Lagos, Lisbon, Santa Maria-Azores, Lajes-Azores, La Palma-Canary Islands, Tenerife, Aruba, St. Martin, Barbados, Dakar, Keflavik, Honolulu, Hilo, Guam, Thailand, Yokota, Japan, Fairbanks, Naples, Okinawa. Some of these destinations were frequent; others were only done once.

Usually we would have two days off at destinations; sometimes we would "Commercial" (buy tickets) to another city to originate a trip. It was an airline of foreign travel for the crews.

At certain times of the year, we were contracted as a sub-service for a foreign air carrier. This was for the Muslim airlift to Mecca, which could not be accommodated by a scheduled airline whose schedule had no flexibility. The two times that I bid monthly trips for this service were for "Royal Air Maroc." We were based in Fez Morocco and operated out of the other major cities to Jeddah to both take them in to and out of Jeddah with a ferry leg in return. Some things were boring, some interesting. The countries of Morocco and Algeria have been technically at war for years, and for this reason, we transit the airspace from Morocco to Algeria as "Overseas National Airways," a U.S. carrier. When leaving Algeria for Libyan airspace, we transit as "Royal Air Moroc" and from Libyan to Egypt and Saudi Arabia as ONA again. This is not a risky deception; it is a face-saving procedure accepted for and by the relative countries to continue air commerce.

The DC-8-63CF was a convertible freighter. It would normally take 24 hours or more and had been accomplished before with a few of the ONA aircraft. On one occasion, the company was hired to fly cows from Toronto, Canada, to Tehran, Iran. The Shaw who was in power at that time wanted to build up a dairy herd, and all the cows were pregnant black & whites. I had a crash pad in Long Beach, New York, for times when I could not get home to Florida, and as I drove along Rockaway Boulevard, I noticed a billboard that had a United Pilot being served a meal in the cockpit while he said, "Sometimes I Think I Fly A Restaurant." I remembered that when I got to my airplane that had just been converted into a barn. Polyurethane came down from where the overheads had been across the windows and where the seats had been over the cargo pallet floor and up the other side. Straw was everywhere; railings had been installed to partition the animals for loading, unloading and en route. This time, I think I am flying a barn. It is a clean barn for now because this is the first flight. I have to go to Toronto where they will load the animals from a field where they were dried out a little for 24 hours. There was a company bulletin that I read while they were loading, and it called for the pilots to make a very small sudden stop just prior to standing up the throttles on takeoff so that the animals would brace themselves naturally. It also suggested a slow rotation to a modified deck angle that probably did not meet criteria. Overall, we were underway very quickly, considering we had 103 pregnant cows we were herding to Frankfurt for a crew change. The first difference I noticed was that, during taxi out, there were tiny little movements fore and aft and left and right that never stopped. The next night we would be picking up the following herd to take to Tehran, and so on. We had two cowboys in the back that would help keep an eye on the cows and help the ground crews during the refueling stop with large fans to keep them cool since the body heat from so many animals is high. There would be no meals served tonight quite like the UAL restaurant advertisement. The day that we took the next section I noticed that a couple of baby cows were tied to the stairs so they do not wander away. They were kept in Germany; I guess they had citizenship by default, but they would probably be trampled if left onboard. The same thing occurred in Tehran, but they went with their moms.

The next time I flew a cargo flight was from Guam to Udapow, Thailand. It was a MAC flight carrying Class A explosive warheads, and the company doubled our life insurance. That was such a relaxing consideration.

Right about this time, I was approached to become an ALPA Committee Chairman by the Local Executive Chairman, Tom Ahern. I loved the guy; he was a big help when I was first starting with ONA, but I kidded him about me being a committee of one. I did not take any company positions and none of the union's offers, which made me a committee of one when it came to telling anyone how the average DC-8 pilot was being affected by either one. He was not amused, and I felt badly for being so offhanded about it. As it turned out, many of the pilots who had been doing this non-paid work for years decided not to run again, and I was talked into running for the LEC, "Local Executive Chairman," and I won. Shortly afterwards, the company closed all other crew bases, and the LEC position became the MEC chairman as well. So now, I was the "Master Executive Chairman." This is a dictator position; no ratification is necessary. Wow, what power; the first thing I decide to do is nothing. That does not last long. Ed Starkloff called me in the office and congratulated me on being MEC. I enquired about what went with this title if I needed to be congratulated. He said, "Well for openers, your trip to Washington for the NMB hearings." "What hearings?" I asked. He described a leftover grievance from months ago that would now be heard before the "National Mediation Board." I listened. I went to my crash pad and called Milt Marshall, the last MEC, my friend and

124

the one who talked me into being the LEC, now MEC. It is a personal thing between a pilot who is on the local committee vs. an executive of the company. I am annoyed that I am just starting out and have old outstanding issues, so I wanted to settle this thing. I asked Starkloff to work on the executive involved so that when we get to the NMB we are able to settle it, which was what happened. Being the MEC entitled me to more contact with the company because not long after I received a call in the middle of the night from Starkloff telling me about an accident in Africa and giving me as much information as he had. I asked him, "What do you want me to do?" He misinterpreted this and said, "I do not want you to do anything. I just have to call you by virtue of you being on a list to call."

As MEC chairman, I, together with Captain Bill Burks, Chief Pilot of the DC-8, flew to London, Abidjan and then to Niamey, Niger. It would not be a pleasant sight. The fuselage was crumpled and still smoking after three days. Some local people were picking through the cargo items and cartons of cigarettes out of the cargo pallets. The left landing gear was severed and located earlier in the wreckage path; the cockpit was separated at the manufacture section and resting upside down. The captain and the flight engineer had been thrown out of the very top of the cockpit, which is a separate section that was found close to their bodies still in their seats, sitting upright with seat and shoulder harnesses still attached. The remarkable thing was the survival of the copilot and loadmaster. The copilot remembered unlocking his seatbelt and falling directly to grass and dirt, then crawled out of the wreckage. The loadmaster was more seriously injured and had to be assisted. They both survived to fly again.

The physical reason for the breakup of the aircraft was caused by a deep ditch that had been dug to pour concrete for mounting approach lights on. The left landing gear had gone into this ditch and precipitated everything that followed. The ditch was approximately 300 feet short of the runway. The aircraft should not have been touching down in this area and the reason remained unknown. The French NTSB had official jurisdiction in this country, and Bob Ramage of the FAA-FSDO office in Minneola, New York, and I were appointed to the FDR and VR recorder project in Paris, and so we left Niger. The tape in that era voice recorder turned to ashes from the heat and the Flight Data Recorder which only recorded five parameters: "Heading," "Altitude," "Airspeed," "Vertical Acceleration," and "Time," and required very experienced people to interpret it. After three days of listening and participating, the best and probably most accurate answer was the very simple French NTSB ruling. "Pilot error," by landing 300 feet short of runway, casual factors, minimum visual conditions, severe damage caused by the ditch construction.

All of which was true but ignored the possibility of wind shear, and did not address the testimony of the Local Representative who was waiting for the aircraft. He said he saw a defused glow of light get slightly brighter near where he would expect the airplane to appear. Then he heard the engines which he thought must be in reverse thrust only much louder than normal and than the aircraft appeared out of the blowing dust, standing nearly on its tail. Being 187 feet long, this would have a difficult position to achieve without power being applied.

I felt that the aircraft was attempting to go around from this situation either before striking the ground or afterward. I also felt that the wing was weakened when the landing gear assembly complete with box construction was torn lose and remained a separate piece of wreckage apart from the main. It is entirely possible that the wing remained intact for the time necessary to become airborne for a few seconds before separating. This would explain the aircraft's height above the ground to appear to be standing on its tail, as the right wing with two operating engines at full power would have yawed the flight path to the left with right wing high and accelerating the fuselage to the ground in a way that the nose-wheel side load twisted the cockpit off catapulting two crew members and seats out of their tracks, through the top of the cockpit leaving the other two crew members hanging upside down and miraculously alive.

The wind shear aspect is possible since the Niamey airport is at the top of a cliff as the flight path comes over the Niger River. The wind shear recovery procedure was Max Power and sacrifice airspeed all the way to intermittent stick shaker before sacrificing altitude. Once below "Landing Ref" speed, it may not be possible to stop descent at Max Landing weight. Nothing I have said here changed the report but explained the difficult conditions and choices they may have encountered before touchdown. Having addressed the rep's statement, which never wavered, I felt that the accident was clearer to me.

Jess Williams never remembered anything about the accident. There were people that thought he was concealing something. The company asked me to suggest Sodium Pentothal. Before I would do that, I investigated with a Doctor Masters who was the leading ALPA Flight Surgeon, and when he got back to me, he had talked with the Air Force and others, none of who would recommend it. He also told me something more important, that Jess Williams had contacted him personally, told him the circumstances, and would like to take Sodium Pentothal to see if it would help him remember.

The Line Check, required once a year by regulation, can produce some real surprises and some interesting laughs when it is over. With ONA, the Chief Pilots and Line Check pilots held a line and flew it to the extent it was possible. Bob Love was the System Chief Pilot and a straightforward guy and good pilot, but he could be confrontational when things were not working the way he wanted or the way that he thought was best for the company. I was the candidate for a line check from Yokota, Japan, to Travis AFB in California. It would usually require refueling at Anchorage, unless we had exceptionally good tailwinds. It was Bob's crew, and they usually flew together when possible. On this day, I was the Captain; he was the Check Airman giving me a check. Gabe Potter was the copilot, and Dave McCloy was the flight engineer. Bob sat in the observer's seat behind me and observed the T.O. climb out to cruise altitude and Inertial Navigational setups and flight plan estimates, and so on. He had not really had much to say to any of us. Hours later, as we approached the Bethel VOR on the Aleutian chain, the first land based Nav-Aid, we would use it to compare the INS accuracy. I put my headset on to quietly check the Morse code. While on that frequency, I caught the Anchorage weather knowing we would land at Anchorage for fuel. Suddenly I was very alert. Anchorage had winds of 30 knots across the runway. In about 15 minutes, we would be over the Bethel VOR where an airway would go direct to Fairbanks or direct to Anchorage. I asked Gabe Potter to check the Fairbanks weather and then recheck the Anchorage weather. He did and handed it to me. Fairbanks was no problem, but somewhat North of Anchorage, which put it further from Travis AFB. I told Gabe to call ATC and get a revised clearance to Fairbanks from overhead Bethel. Bob heard that, if he had not heard anything else, and jumped up and said, "What are you doing?" I explained and he said that I had been doing a good job but that now I was screwing up. I told Gabe to get on the radio. Gabe looked distressed. Bob finally said, "Wait a minute; do you know what the crosswind limitation is for this aircraft?" I replied, "25 knots." "Hmm," he said, "look, I'll take it in there and you can get the landing down at Travis; that will complete your check ride." I refused, and we went to Fairbanks, refueled, and proceeded to Travis. Bob did not have much to say. Bob is an old-timer from the WW2 era, and I used to pull the gear for him on the DC-7s. I knew him well, and I had seen him hassle pilots in ways that make them better pilots, and for all I knew, that was what he was doing, but I was not going to start a conversation with him if I did not have to. I told Gabe to contact the company and advised them of our intentions and to get a new flight plan for departing Fairbanks. Gabe looked to where Bob was sitting but called in my request. We transited Fairbanks without the need to clear customs since we left the troops onboard and we were only going to be 30 minutes late at Travis AFB.

At Travis AFB after the GIs were off the airplane, we deplaned. Bob was already out on the ramp talking to a friend, a Seaboard World Captain who came off a DC-8 in front of us. We all started to walk into the terminal. Dave McCloy, the Flight Engineer, and I are directly behind these two old veterans and we heard the Seaboard Pilot say, "Did you hear about the SAS DC-8 in Anchorage?" Bob turned to him and said no. "Well they landed there and got an outboard engine pod on the ground and the airport is still closed."

Bob said, "Well they obliviously do not know the limitations of their aircraft; since we knew they had a 30 knot crosswind, we went to Fairbanks." McCloy chuckled and hit me in the ribs with his elbow. I guess I passed the line check.

ONA had navigators until 1972, and so I had the experience for three years of working with these dedicated people. They had a separate seniority list, and like the flight engineers were separate from the pilot list. I mention this because a number of scheduled airlines had a pilot qualified crew member in these positions who would be eligible to progress into the pilots' positions.

The navigators were responsible for the over-water navigation so only out of range of land based Nav-Aids were they paid. However, like the pilots, many pre-flight duties take place. The pilot's pay starts at aircraft movement.

At waypoint positions, they would pass a card up to the front for the pilots to work with. The pilot flying would make the noted correction to the heading of the aircraft, and the other pilot would make the necessary position report to the land-based facility in control of the airspace. On the North

Atlantic, there were only two controlling agencies, "Gander" and "Shanwick," the latter being a composite for Shannon, Ireland and Prestwick, Scotland.

Celestial navigation is only as accurate as the correctness of the time that you have. For that reason the navigator would always have the pilots tune in the HF frequency of the atomic clock facilities, one being the Navel Observatory. The navigator had other equipment available to him such as Loran and the pilots who could use the weather radar, NDBs, some of which are very long distance and Doppler ground speed readouts, which was probably the best part of that technology.

The camaraderie between the pilots and navigators was sometimes honed with accusations of incompetence of one for the other. Annoyances of being given a one-degree heading change or too many heading changes included responses such as:

"A one degree change cannot even be read on the compass."

"Then make a ten degree change and nine back."

"You have given us four heading changes in four minutes."

"Sorry I was going around a gravy spot on my chart."

The beginning of the end for the navigators began in early 1972 with the Designation of ONA as one of the trial airlines to run proving flights with the Litton Inertial Navigation Units. We were chosen because of our random worldwide flying. A triple installation of Litton 51 Inertial Navigation systems were installed, Left and Right forward Pedestals and one overhead. A Litton Representative would fly with each equipped aircraft who would observe and advise the pilots who have already been through a ground school on the operation and checked out. An ONA navigator was still assigned to the flight and was in charge of over-water navigation. We did not engage the autopilot system to the INS systems but observed their readouts just the same. After 30 days of operating this way, we engaged the systems and with an approved check airman, we each qualified before being approved without a navigator onboard.

The Navigators were all given a severance pay and let go. I am sure many of them had gone through the ups and downs of the non-sked business before, but this was different. This was a profession that was coming to an end permanently. For a few that had retired from other airlines before coming to ONA, it was nothing new. Navigator E. Blackburn formally of Pan American Airways and better known as "Blacky" was small in stature but tall in reputation; word had it that he had been Chief Navigator for PAA.

My first trip using the INS entirely on my own was from Athens to New York. After crossing the North Atlantic, we were proceeding to overhead the radio beacon on Anacosta Island, in the Gulf of the Saint Lawrence. The needle on the ADF was hesitant about which way it would swing around, going slightly left, then right, etc. This was an indication of being directly overhead. The art of navigation had transitioned to the pilots.

In 1973, ONA placed two new DC-10-30CF aircraft in the fleet, making the transition to wide-body aircraft of the new era. They stayed with the philosophy of Convertible Freighters for military preference in contract awards, which for a non-sked could be the difference between profit and loss.

The scheduled airlines would not invest to do this because of the penalty of higher weights of stronger decks, landing gear, large cargo doors, etc., which would affect their profits on everyday flying. We carried 380 Passengers on DC-10s, all in coach configuration since the packaged charters of the leading sales groups worldwide were interested in the profit margins of the transportation, in addition to the hotels, the tours, etc. This was also true for the DC-8s, which carried 254 passengers. Only now do you hear of passenger numbers of this magnitude because of the advances in Jet Engine Thrust, which allows comfort and great weights. The thrust of the DC-8-63 Jet Engines was 19,000 lbs x four engines = total thrust of 76,000 lbs. The Thrust of the Jet Engine on the New Boeing 777 is now approaching 130,000 lbs of Thrust per engine x two engines = 260,000 lbs. Using the word "Thrust" interchangeable with Horsepower is not scientifically accurate but is not an unreasonable comparison.

There were times in the 1950s and 1970s that ONA carried more passengers on the North Atlantic than Pan American Airways, and ONA individual flights during most of those two decades were always carrying greater numbers of passengers than the scheduled airlines.

In November 1975 we were going to position several aircraft to Jeddah for the beginning of Ramadan, the Islamic Religion's annual airlift to and from Mecca. I had usually flown these trips whether I wanted to or not by virtue of my seniority, but this year instead of a hotel in Jeddah, ONA had leased a cruise ship for that thirty-day period, which would be anchored in the Red Sea just offshore. For this reason the trips went very senior, and I did not have to go.

Living in a crash pad in Long Beach, New York, close to JFK, I knew of two flight attendants that wanted a ride to the airport that day so they would not have to leave their cars at the airport for a month. I had agreed beforehand, and so when the day came, I drove over and picked them up. I dropped them off at the ONA office, and there were dozens of crew members with all their long duration luggage awaiting company buses that could take them to the aircraft. This would be a ferry flight with just crews onboard.

An hour or so later back at my apartment, I was eating lunch and watching the television, when they suddenly broke in with news. "A Charter Airline Jet has crashed at JFK airport, and at this time we have no reports of survivors." Ohhh no, I looked out the back door, which was in the direction of the airport and a huge boiling black cloud was readily visible here on the island. I had this horrible feeling that I had just delivered those two young girls to their deaths. Shortly, the television was including the name of the airline, an Overseas National DC-10. I was already closing the door to leave because it could not have been anyone else.

I drove to the JFK Medical Center, which was built there for just this reason, but kept busy with the medical needs of all the employees at the airport in addition. I found the crew members either there or arriving, and none were hurt so far. No one was hurt except one of the cockpit crew who went down an "Escape Tape" and burned his hands sliding too fast. All together, there were 10 working crew and 129 deadheading crew. The aircraft was destroyed by fire.

The accident was caused by birds on the runway. These birds were seagulls, not normal seagulls, but birds that lived on the dumps that exist not far from the airport and were closer in size to turkeys.

Several of these birds had been sitting on the runway and were ingested by the number three engine, causing an explosion of that engine and a resulting wing fire long before the aircraft was stopped. The educated evacuation by all passengers being trained crew members prevented casualties.

As if this was not enough, shortly after the New Year 1976, we lost another DC-10 in Istanbul, Turkey. The flight was en route to Ankara, and then upon arriving found the weather below landing minimums. Going to the alternate airport, Istanbul, they discovered the runway lights were on, but on the shortest runway. After several conversations about this, and then being told that someone had to return to the airport to change this situation, they realized that fuel was now the number one consideration and attempted a landing on the short runway. In the process of taking advantage of all of the runway, the pilot tried to place the landing gear on the very end but a rise was in that area and ripped the landing gear off. The aircraft slid to a stop with the cockpit shutting everything off that might start a fire while the cabin crew evacuated 380 passengers without injury. The aircraft was a total loss, however.

Overseas National had ordered three more DC-10s after that, but growing talk of airline deregulation seemed to be a growing unknown entity. Airline operating certificates, once a very valuable asset, were not even on the balance sheet anymore.

At the pilot level, we had no knowledge of the consternation that existed in the executive offices of any of the airlines, least of all our company.

In the offices of the M.E.C., that was I, I had everything delegated that could be delegated and dealt only with things that were out of the ordinary. Starkloff called me in the office and said that they have been sending random FDR units to one of the major airlines for readouts. He asked, "Do you have a problem with this?"

"Not on the surface, but why?"

"Well they do it for their pilots."

"Do their pilots have a problem with it?"

"No because it eliminates some part of the check rides."

"Will we have that benefit?"

"No."

"Where are we really going with this conversation?"

"Captain Frank Foster and Joe Norman ferried a flight to Boston and shot six approaches and never broke out and then returned to New York."

"Makes sense to me."

"Well this FDR was sent out for evaluation, and it seems that they started each approach 1500 feet too high at the final approach fix and never got to decision height."

"So you're saying that they were about 3000 feet at the outer marker instead of about 1500 feet, is that right?"

"Yes."

"And they did this six times?"

"Yes."

"What was the weather in New York when they returned?"

"IFR at about 300 feet."

"And they got in okay?"

"Yes."

"The manufacture of that recorder is the same as from the crash in Africa, is that right?"

"Yes."

"Send it to them."

"I did, same thing."

"Hmm, I'll talk to them about this without all this FDR stuff or our conversation, okay?"

"Make it quick. I do not want them flying again until I know."

I called Frank, and he said yes that it was real low and they never saw the runway and besides, "I let Joe fly all the approaches since the copilots do not get enough of the real low ones." I asked him about the altitude at the outer marker and he said whatever was published, 1500 feet or so. I told him the company was suspicious. He laughed. I did also and told him I would be in touch. I went back to Starkloff with what I was told.

"What do you think?" "I think they are telling the truth." "Not good enough." "I want to send this to ALPA." "No way this is leaving the office."

"Starkey, I will take personal responsibility for its return."

"What do you think they can do?"

"They have a guy, Harold Martheson, who is probably the most respected expert in the country on these FDRs."

"Make it quick and get it back here."

About a week later, I am in the office with Starky again. "Well, did you bring it back?" "Yes and with a letter that says that both those companies screwed it up by a factor of two." Starky said, "It is unbelievable that could happen." I believe that major airline gave us a lot of heartburn and expense for our money, and that the policy they had in place was probably suspect now, even for their own purposes. The strange part was the manufacturer being careless as well. The bottom line to this event was that the airline admitted their error and the manufacturer admitted they were led into the same error by the airline. Both the airline and the manufacturer followed with letters that I copied to the pilots involved.

I returned to flying by picking up the next part of my line that was available. A trip from JFK to Frankfurt, it felt like home to me. I loved the Nasserhof Hotel in Wiesbaden, the people, and oh yes, the food and the music of the piano player that came into the restaurant at 1600 hrs. The Mosel wine. I liked to hide from being an American just to indulge myself in their enjoyment. Raising your eyebrows for "Yes," shaking your head for "No," or shrugging your shoulder for "Whatever" would allow you to tread water for a little while. One evening, a beautiful woman sat down a couple of barstools away. Dressed elegantly in expensive clothes and jewelry, she smiled and then turned to the bartender who treated her with great respect. They only spoke in German. I ordered another Mosel, in English. As he served it, he said, "Ah, you're American. The lady had asked me. I wasn't sure. You are on holiday?" "No ONA." "Ah a pilot?" "Yes, and she is a very pretty lady." "Yes very...a lady of the evening." "Hmm, no thanks." Just then, two flight attendants came in from shopping and plopped down on either side of me. One asked me if I was trolling. I mentioned that it appeared to be working; there were three now.

"Buy us a drink and we will let you know."

"I am presuming that you are going to say yes, so I am going to say no!...Now I will buy you drinks, knowing I am wasting my time and my money."

CHAPTER 10

Airline Deregulation

Dispatch called me at my crash pad, and I answered ready to sound like a recording, in case it was crew scheduling. I only did this as a joke, and they would say, "Come on Flavell; we know it's you." It was dispatch telling me that Mr. Bailey had left a message in my mail folder to see him ASAP and had advised them to tell me if they saw me. Sam Rogers said he was just giving me a heads up, and I thanked him.

The Negotiations Committee had been warning me about how the company would try to get me in their pocket before contract time, now that it was 1978 and up for renewal and to be careful since I did not have much experience with this sort of thing. That is why I had the committees in place to handle these things anyhow.

I checked my mail folder first, but then started toward the second floor but was stopped by two members who warned me again about talking directly to Bailey about the contract.

I knew Bill Bailey back in 1962 when he was Chairman of NACA, an association of non-skeds, and I had always admired his straight talk, so I was not worried, and besides I had enough confidence in myself not to commit the pilots to anything before talking to the rest of the leaders.

Bill got right to the point. "George, I just wanted to give you some information upfront so you will not feel like I went around you or the pilots. The news will be in the *Journal* tomorrow or the next day, and that is this: we are going out of business sometime this year, perhaps as soon as six months, but probably more like eight or ten months."

"What can the pilots do to prevent that from happening?"

"I wish that were the issue, George; it is a business decision made by the two largest principals in the company. We do not feel that we can compete in a business that is headed for a bloodbath of competition with deregulation, and the irony of the two crashes that we have had has actually improved our financial position due to the replacement value insurance figure. However, if we stay in business, our insurance rates will now escalate, assuming they will continue to insure us, and the real hammer coming down is the delayed delivery of the next DC-10, which because of a Douglas strike has delayed the delivery beyond the season of our most lucrative months."

"What if we work for nothing?"

"I wish it was that easy."

"We are going to give the pilots a raise, however, for the remaining duration."

"I will not accept that."

"What?"

"I will not accept it."

"You cannot do that; the pilots will hang you."

"Maybe, but as MEC, I do not need ratification and the answer is you cannot change our contract unilaterally."

"I have to get our VP Karl Wernett in here to listen to this."

"Hi, George."

"Good morning, Karl."

Bill reviewed the previous conversation for Karl.

Karl, smiling, said, "The company could get big headlines for these kind of labor discussions."

"Karl, from the union's standpoint, we could probably grab a headline or two also, but my concern is tying together the notice of 'Going Out of Business' with 'Pilots Get Raise.' "

"It has the connotation for the pilots to appear callous to the company's situation, and that more money always fixes things with them."

Bill spoke up, "What would you suggest?"

"Make it a severance, a bonus, or a held back incentive to remain flying for the company until everything is wound down, since I sense that is the reason behind this."

Bill said, "I thank you for that, and we will consider doing it that way; thanks for coming in. One other favor, if you would keep this confidential until it is in the paper since there are many employees to consider. I just wanted to make sure you were prepared to answer questions for the pilots."

I went downstairs where a few people wanted to know what was going on; it was amazing watching the grapevine in progress. I told them that the company and I were far apart on a new contract. I offered the pilots' services free of charge, and they demanded that pilots have a raise instead, and I refused. We all laughed. It was not really funny, and that statement was only too true.

The news came out in the *Wall Street Journal* two days later, and some of them did not believe that either, saying it was a ploy they had used before. Most employees were stunned; only the pilots who would be hurt the worst would have the small groups of doubters either for their own morale or because of something in past negotiations, but this was a blockbuster and not a threat that had a remedy.

A few months later, many were saying we needed to sit down and negotiate with the company.

The next few months, copilots were being furloughed; captains were now flying copilot, and eventually captains were being furloughed. September held a lot of "Lasts."

Early on, I had contacted Jerry McCabe, my old instructor on the DC-9 at Douglas Aircraft Company, to find out whom I could contact for employment there. He said, "You might start with me. I am the Chief Pilot now." I asked if I should hang up and start over with a little more respect in my voice. He thought that was a splendid idea but a little late. He hired me subject to paperwork that would go back and forth, and I planned to start on August 1, 1978. I would fly my last trip with ONA as a copilot for my close friend, Milt Marshall, on a DC10 trip to JFK. After the parking checklist was complete, we delayed leaving the cockpit so the passengers would not see two grown men trying to control tears that somehow just appeared.

The next day I turned in all my company material including my DOD card, which each pilot had for MAC flights. I glanced at it one last time. I liked the statement on the back that said, "Assimilated Rank: Major through Colonel."

Milt Marshall would fly his last trip in September of 1978 as reported by C.V. Glines in "Death of an Airline," *Airline Pilot Magazine*, January 1979. The story follows:

Capt. Jack Hogan braked the Overseas National Airways DC-10 to a stop in front of the Military Airlift Command terminal at McGuire Air Force Base, N.J. It was a few minutes after 11 p.m. last September 13. The 303 military passengers and dependants who had boarded at Frankfurt, West Germany, filed off and proceeded through customs, unaware that they had become a final statistic in the history of an airline. The flight-routine, professional and on schedule, was ONA's last revenue operation. ONA was officially out of business as of that date.

Also aboard were 10 deadheading flight deck and cabin crew members who had flown the final eastbound leg from Charleston, S.C. to Frankfurt. They lingered a short while chatting with the active crew who later ferried the aircraft back to its home base at Kennedy International Airport.

There was a little laughter among the group, but, as the significance of the final revenue landing took hold, many tears were shed quietly. Some deadheading crew members, seeking to avoid the hassle of going home from Kennedy, chose to take a limousine from McGuire to their respective destinations. It is also suspected they wanted to avoid the really final landing at Kennedy when the close friendships born of working together in the air for many years would become only a memory.

Capt. Milton F. Marshall, former ONA Master Executive Council chairman and director of flight operations, who bid the first officers position on the last eastbound flight, lingered a bit. When the other crew members were out of sight, he handed me (I had flown jump seat on both legs) the metal wings from his uniform.

"Here," he said, "I won't be needing these anymore." We shook hands and he walked off into the darkness. It was the final moment in a live drama that had, by that small gesture, played itself out.

In its relatively short history, ONA, one of the nations 10 supplemental airlines, had hit economic highs as well as lows. At one time, it had been "the biggest and most respected nonsked airline in the business," according to one observer, and claimed that it flew more international passenger miles than any other U.S. Carrier with the exception of Pan Am.

Founded in 1950, ONA began charter operations at Oakland, Calif., with five DC-4s. It then fought its way to the top during the early days of fiercely competitive bidding for military airlift contracts. From 1955 to 1957, the young airline participated in the evacuation of Dutch nationals from Indonesia, the emigration of Hungarian refugees, the delivery of to strikebound Iceland and the transport of supplies to the French fighting in Vietnam. By 1957, ONA could boast that its aircraft and crews had flown a distance equal to 1000 times around the globe.

142

In the summer of 1958, after accumulating transoceanic experience, ONA began flying four DC-6s on group charters to Europe. The next year it began to carry out one of the largest Military Air Transport Service contracts ever awarded a single carrier up to that time. Twelve DC-7s and one DC-6 were added to the fleet and operations began over both oceans in support of military forces.

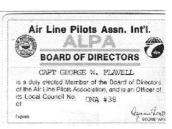

Air Line Pilots Assn. Int'l.

BOARD OF DIRECTORS

CAPT. GEORGE W. FLAVELL

is a duly elected Member of the Board of Directors of the Air Line Pilots Association, and is an Officer of its Local Council No. ONA #38 of

Expires

J. W. Bailey, President

OVERSEAS NATIONAL AIRWAYS

July 13, 1978

Dear George:

The decision to suspend its charter operations was an extremely difficult one for ONA and one that was made with a very deep sense of regret. Notwithstanding what our counterparts in the supplemental industry may be doing, ours is a sound decision and made of necessity.

I want to express my sincere appreciation for your loyal support and assistance, not only to me personally, but to all of the management and support personnel at ONA. A Captain's responsibility is an enormous one and we take great pride in the loyalty, dedication and professional competence that you have demonstrated during your many years with the Company.

We are particularly appreciative of the key role you have played as MEC during this recent period. Your sense of responsibility to the pilot group has been matched by your consideration for the Company's best interests.

I will miss all of the associations I've enjoyed during the years that we have worked together and all of us at ONA join in wishing you much deserved success in the future.

Sincerely,

Bill

Captain George Flavell
Overseas National Airways
JFK International Airport
Jamaica, New York 11430

AIR LINE PILOTS ASSOCIATION, INT'L

CAPT. GEORGE W. FLAVELL
CHAIRMAN ONA COUNCIL 36
MASTER EXECUTIVE CHAIRMAN ONA

SUITE 508, EXPRESSWAY BLDG.
91-31 QUEENS BLVD.
ELMHURST, NEW YORK 11373

OFFICE: (212) 671-5300
HOME: (516) 421-3988

John F. Kennedy International Airport; Jamaica, New Y...

143

In Long Beach, California, I had a retired U.S. Navy Admiral sent to accompany me from the hotel to the offices of Douglas Aircraft. Since he knew I had been hired over the phone, he asked me how I knew Captain McCabe, the Chief Pilot, and I replied, "He was my instructor on the DC-9-32CF about 11 years ago." He asked me what aircraft I had flown in the service. My answer was to tell him that the U.S. Air Force would not let an airman 2nd class fly their airplanes. He wondered aloud why I would be chosen to be a DC-10 Production Test Pilot. I ventured, "Because I am rated and experienced in that aircraft, with considerable international experience and over 20,000 hours of large aircraft time." He said, "Welcome aboard."

Accompanying me into Jerry's office, we talked a little while, and then Jerry turned me over to an old friend of mine from ONA that had joined Douglas a few months earlier. It was Boyd Michael who actually was my Chief Pilot on Log Air when we were based out of Wright Patterson AFB. Boyd had the reputation of getting to the bottom of things quickly, and he proved it again. He took me down to the flight line and got me a locker, a flight suit, a badge, charts and numerous other things. He introduced me to other pilots, got me a desk near his, and briefed me on the official procedures and the usual daily routines. If not flying or resting from a previous flight, we were expected in the office at 9 a.m. What transpired after that was either up to you if you had some project assigned or something you wanted to research. We had access to all facilities, simulators, Carrousel Self Training Grounds Schools on all current Douglas aircraft. We were required to keep ourselves current on the aircraft type we were assigned to. I went through the machine shop and watched the computerized milling machines and others marveling at how much the modern machine shop work had changed. I wandered over to a flight simulator that tested limited parameters of electrics, hydraulics, engine failures and braking. Poking around over there, someone called me Captain, and I thought someone knew me, but it was the badge I was wearing that identified me as a company pilot. Since it did not show what I did, I asked how he knew that. He laughed and said the large black bar on it. Does that mean covert activities? I was kidding because at Lockheed some aircraft were painted black. He said, "You know, maybe that was the company's point when they changed all the pilots to black." I said, "I do not understand." "He said, "Well the pilots tried to form a union a few years ago and failed. After that, they wore black badges versus the different colors you see on the others." "Thank you for the history lesson, and I'll stop by again." "Do that and we'll get you in the simulator here to practice Rejected Takeoffs." "Okay, I definitely will be back soon."

Going back to the office, I noticed all of the pilots were gone. Roger Conant came out of his office and introduced himself and said, "I guess you do not play golf?" I confessed that that was true and asked if he played. He said, "No but I wish I did." "Why is that?" I inquired." He said, "If I played golf, I could come in at 9 a.m. and tell the secretaries I am going to building 41 and go play golf with the rest of these guys, so now I've told you the office protocol, at least I will expect to see you here." I asked him if I reported to him. He said, "No, not to me, in fact, I don't know who I report to, and I have been here thirty years. I usually wait until someone tells me to do something, and then I just do it. It is really hectic at times because someone will be appointed as Project Manager for something, and for that period they have the whip, and if they pick you, then you will go wherever. You are ONA, I know, and they like ONA pilots around here; they are competent and have such worldwide experience. They will file their own international flight plans and just make things work. I will tell you that they are in a crunch for a DC-10 Captain for Nigerian Airways. I heard that today, and Stan Forster is the Project Manager; you would be based in London and fly from there to Lagos and then to New York and back. Probably two or three times a month. Would that be something you would like?" "Sure,

I'm interested." "Okay, I will mention it to Stan. So many of the pilots live here and do not like to commute or go offshore."

Stan found me the next morning, and as we talked the more interested I became. He was pleased that I had so much international experience, plus the North African flying, and when I told him I had flown in and out of Lagos one time, he made his mind up.

"I need you to go and live in London for at least three months, maybe more, and after that, we have a longer-term situation where I would need you in Singapore. How do you feel about that?" "Sounds good to me. I lived in the Philippines for two years." "Great, I have to get you some Nigerian Airways DC-10 Manuals and Procedures, and you will need a simulator check ride using their procedures. Your crew will usually be all Nigerian; however, we do have some Douglas Flight Engineers in their system. After the check ride, you can fly on your U.S. license for 30 days, but you will need to make a special trip to Lagos for a Nigerian ATP. There is a physical and a Civil Aviation Written Test, based on the old English Test, which is not easy, but there is a lot of wiggle room." "Why do they not check out more Nigerian captains?" I asked. "They need experienced pilots for insurance reasons, and they will be grounded if pilots like yourself are not available, and of course, we could not sell airplanes to them if we cannot provide the necessary cockpit support, among other things."

The next day I picked up the manuals, told the secretaries I was going to building 41, and went to my hotel to study. The following day I took a check ride, using their procedures as well as performing all of the necessary maneuvers, approaches, missed approaches, engine failures, and other abnormal and emergency procedures that I would need to successfully bring my U.S. six-month currency check up close to the date that I would be leaving the country. Douglas did this so they would not have to bring you back to the U.S.

just for that purpose. Within a couple of days, I was on my way to London, and once there, I headed for Curzon Street that was near the "Green Park Station" on the Tube for getting to Heathrow. I found a fourth-floor walkup that was 1200 U.S. dollars a month, and it was an expense account item, so it was not too bad. The Playboy Club was just up the street and also Hyde Park with good Italian and Indian restaurants close by.

The next day, Stan called and said he would take me to the British Airways Uniform Location that would issue my Nigerian Uniform. I met him at the bottom of the walkup, and we caught a taxi. The uniform location was not prominent but large. It was almost like a Fun Land event in boot camp except for the haircut. The Standard issue was quite a bit. For openers I got two pair of shoes. Stan had asked me to get him a pair, but his size was the next larger size, and I told the man I needed that because my feet swell. I got a uniform jacket, two pair of trousers, stockings, shirts, epilates, ties, hat, and a choice of raincoats—a London Fog with removable liner or a thick-filled raincoat that would be warm. I chose the first. When he finally said, "That is it, sir." I was tempted to ask about underwear.

I gave Stan his shoes, and he helped me carry this load to a taxi, then he dropped me at my flat. I was scheduled to fly out in two days. I had Nigerian-issued charts, which were really from Amsterdam. I would be going to Lagos via Kano. The crew names were all Nigerian. There would be an overnight in Lagos, staying right at the airport hotel. The next night I would fly to Accra, Ghana, Roberts Field, Monrovia, and then on to JFK with three days in New York, then back to London, via the reverse. Stan went with me on the second one and gave me a check ride to New York. On the reverse flight, I got off in Lagos, and Stan rode through to London with another check ride. I stayed an extra day there to take my written exam for a Nigerian License plus get a physical. I was told to make sure that they broke open a new seal for a hypodermic or not let them use it otherwise.

The other helpful item was to blow up the accordion-type bellows, which they timed, seeing how long you could hold it. Sticking your tongue against the inflation tube, you could hold it to record levels, but it was best to give up after about a minute and look winded.

Passing the medical exam, I was off to the Director of Aviations Office for a written test. The director looked very stern, but his secretary was friendly. Finally, after several minutes, I was given the test. The questions were like: which side of the road do you fly if navigating by visual contact? It was a very long test. Finally, the time was up before I finished, and the secretary took it into the director. After a long time, he called me into his office and said he was very sorry, but I had failed. I apologized for failing but thanked him for his kindness. He asked me what Douglas Aircraft would do with me. I told him that I would have to return to California where they would have another assignment for me. He said, "When are you going to fly again?" I said, "I am scheduled to fly this evening's flight back to London." "Oh," he said, "let me look at some of the questions you missed." He reviewed about four questions and with some coaching, I corrected my answers. Finally, he said, "See, I knew you knew the answers; you probably did not read the questions properly and now you have passed the test." I thanked him for his generosity, and we shook hands.

That night, sitting in the cockpit waiting for the last few passengers, a flight attendant came in and said that the Director of Aviation of Nigeria was onboard and would like to come into the cockpit. The other crew members looked shocked, but I could see him waiting behind her, and I said, "By all means, the Director is very welcome to come into the cockpit." As he came in, he shook my hand, as he said that he had business in London tomorrow and how nice it was to see me again. With that, he turned to the others and said, "Gentlemen, have a nice flight," and returned to the cabin.

For about three months, I flew these trips about two or three times a month, and for every day on flight duty, I would earn 50 Naira a day per diem paid by a purser onboard the aircraft. Though I was salaried by Douglas, I was entitled to the daily expense of this amount for each day that I flew. This is true with other foreign airlines as well. The problem with the Naira was that you were not supposed to have more than 50 Naira on your person coming into the country, and you are not allowed to take more than 50 Naira out of the country. This per-diem allotment put us in violation every time we transited the country. The other ex-patriots just put it in their socks, but I still had visions of being hauled off to a Nigerian jail. I collected quite a bit over the weeks that I was in London, and I do not recall the exchange rate, but I do remember the flap I caused when I took it to a London Bank. I was invited into a manager's office where I was asked how I had accumulated so much of this currency. I said, "What are we talking about here? Is this worth so much that we need to discuss how I got it?" The man said, "No sir, but you are only allowed to bring 50 Naira into the country at a time, and this would have taken several trips." "So it took several trips; what is the big deal? Can I convert it to spendable usable currency or not?" "Yes sir, you can, but I have to fill out a form, and you have to sign this form for each 50 Naira." "Oh okay, I am sorry, but I had no idea that this limitation even existed outside their country." I then explained my position and how I came by this money, which I had not seen the need to do before. The amount of English currency I received in exchange I do not even remember; however, the time spent getting it I will never forget.

I remember the short stop we would make in Accra, Ghana, for the sadness that I felt. Armed guards would come to the top of the loading stairs at the main aircraft entrance to prevent hungry people from coming aboard to beg for food. The flight attendants would give some to the guards, which probably did not find its way to anyone else.

The next stop, slightly longer en route, was to Monrovia, Liberia. Roberts Field was the airport's name, and the services and conditions here were much better. Cape Verde Islands and Bermuda were islands that we would come within diversion range en route to New York. The route would be reversed, but we would skip some stations based on company needs laid out before departure. There was a weekly stop in Rome, rather than in Kano, that was in the normal schedule.

Once back in Heathrow, I would wear my raincoat, pack my hat in my suitcase, and look like any other person riding the Tube to Green Park.

My assignment was up almost before I knew it; just one more roundtrip to New York, and I would be heading back to the Beach as the Douglas veterans called it, Long Beach, California.

On this trip, the beginning of a sequence of funny occurrences began. I was standing in the main terminal at Heathrow waiting for the Jet-Way door to open to allow my access to the aircraft. I was in no hurry; I had all the weather information and flight planning material in my flight bag. I happened to notice a Pan American pilot by himself, and he seemed to be looking at me. Soon he walked over and said, "Are you an American?" I nodded and he said, "I think I know you. Were you with ONA?" and I said yes. Then he mentioned the "Digs" bar in Long Beach, New York, and a mutual friend, Wayne Hargis, and so on. Then he stopped suddenly and said, "What is that Elephant on your hat?" I explained that I was flying for Nigerian Airways. "What equipment are you flying?" I said I was flying a DC-10. "Geez, you sure made a successful bounce after ONA, captain and all. Where are you living?" and I said here, and just then, he said, "I have to run; there's my captain." I would see him again some months later, halfway around the world, and I would be wearing another uniform.

Landing much later in Lagos, I stayed with the aircraft because I wanted to talk to the outbound captain. I had been given the aircraft with the center landing gear retracted. It had a damaged brake disc assembly and was dispatched under the M.E.L. (Minimum Equipment Limitations), which details anything that has to be done differently, or limitations on speed, weight, altitude, or whether it has to be repaired within a certain period. This case tonight affected the weight. The maximum takeoff weight must be reduced by 50,000 lbs. The director of operations asked me if it could go nonstop to New York; that was their plan this trip. I told him no, because that 50,000 lbs was coming right out of the fuel. He was thinking of a stop at Dakar and went inside. I sat in the cockpit and planned a trip with a fuel stop at Santa Maria, Azores. That was much better.

The Douglas pilot came in. It was Roger Conant on his retirement flight. I knew he was deadheading in to fly his last flight before age 60 and was the reason I waited to be there, considering the aircraft condition. He was genuinely happy to see me, and I wished him well, but he said he still had an office job and that I would be working for him along with some other pilots. He set his flight bag and travel bag down and took off his jacket, as he peered into the cockpit while hanging it up in a closet. Turning back to me, he smiled and said, "How's the airplane?" I said, "It's fine except the center gear is MEL in the up position." The smile disappeared, and I could tell he was trying to remember something. "Doesn't that call for a weight penalty?" His eyes were looking at something other than where they were pointed. "Hell, that's a big weight penalty." "Yes it is," I said, "50,000 lbs to be exact." "Geez George, how can you bring me this problem on my last flight? Where in hell am I going to get fuel?" He was not as worried as he let on, but he milked it for all it was worth. "Santa Maria, Azores," I said.

"The Azores, a few little islands in the middle of the Atlantic Ocean, and I have to find the correct one." "A real piece of cake old man, and the good news is if you let the passengers off, and I highly recommend you do, they will give the captain a large bottle of Mateus wine. The duty-free shop is open 24 hours." About this time the Director of Operations came in and said, "Oh Captain Conant, I am glad you are here. I have measured the distance to Dakar, and I think you should go there for fuel." Roger said, "Captain Flavell here thinks I should go to Santa Maria Azores." "Oh yes that would be better, but I haven't found a way to get the distance correctly." I mentioned, "I took it off the INS system and you can use Lajes Field as the alternate, a U.S. Air Force Base. I will help you flight plan it and the next leg to JFK." Roger and I followed the director into operations.

My assignment ended the next week, and finally I was back at "The Beach." Roger was glad to see me and said that the flight had gone smoothly, even to the bottle of wine, and he said it really gave a little spice to his last flight. He thanked me for hanging around to help out.

I was reading the paper, drinking coffee, and waiting for 9 a.m. when all the news for the day would be exchanged and some would bug off somewhere and others had assignments. Mine today was to get acquainted with a production flight test. There was a "World Airways" DC-10 going out tomorrow on its first and perhaps only flight test. I was to fly copilot and get familiar with the routine. I got an overview of what it would entail, including the fact the flight test would take most of the day. There would be two flight engineers onboard, and there would be several people in the cabin doing various tests—everything that would be touched on a normal flight, light switches to air vents, signs, audio and PA, lavatories required, fire fighting equipment, emergency exit doors, galleys, ovens, racks, doors and locks. Their lists were several pages long.

Now, the next day, it was taking place as I had read it. In the cockpit, there were thick manuals, with one engineer reading, and the cockpit normal positions responding and replying. It would take one hour before we began to start engines and the better part of another hour before they were all started, one hour to taxi to the runway, and four to six hours of flight tests.

Taxiing to the runway involved turning off different hydraulic pumps and sources and the same with electrical switches and power sources, all the while actuating a systematic range of manual or automatic standby or emergency selections, according to the book man's dictation of must see this value or that result should not indicate this value.

Some of the hydraulic tests required the nose wheel to be turned fully in each direction so that a DC-10 coming out of the factory looked like it was being controlled by someone who had no idea of what they were doing, which was only partially the case with me there. The same procedures were applied to instruments that should be working or not working and that associated warning lights and instrument flags are appearing or not appearing as scheduled. One of the interesting things that I was unprepared for was the simulated engine failure of pulling the thrust lever to idle on takeoff. It is not a big deal; I have done it many times training students in aircraft before the simulator was approved for that maneuver. I knew we would be doing this during the flight test, but I did not think we would be doing it on the very first takeoff this new airplane was making. I do not consider myself a super conservative pilot by any means, and I was always suspicious of anyone that was, since they seemed to get in more trouble being afraid of everything than the ones who make things work. I was very careful when I had passengers to protect, but I was capable of making more ambitious decisions always with an alternate plan when I was alone, or with a crew I would consult. I do not have any superstitions or habits I always have to follow, but I would not have pulled an engine back on an aircraft that had never been in the air before. What we were doing here is referred to as "Production Flight Test," and we wear Blue Flight

Suits. The pilots that certify takeoff distances, landing distances and all other aspects of original certification are referred to as "Engineering Flight Test" and wear "Orange Flight Suits." The easiest way to look at the difference is that Blue Suits are checking things to see if they work as advertised; the Orange Suits take things to the braking point to determine the maximum limit.

We were at altitude now, and one of the tests would be turning off the individual air conditioning packs, which would allow a check of each pack's function. The next check would be to turn all packs off and note the rate that the cabin would climb (lose pressurization).

The engineer turned to me and said, "You're an experienced airline pilot; how fast would you think it might climb?" I asked him, "With or without the outflow valve closed?" "Oh yeah, good question, with the outflow valve closed." I said, "About 3000 feet per minute." He said, "Watch," as he turned off the packs and the cabin was climbing just under 1000 feet per minute. He smiled and said, "See, you can learn something doing something you never get a chance to do." I did not want to challenge his tutoring, but I did mention that if he tried that on an aircraft with twenty thousand flight cycles on it, he might learn something too, providing he grabbed his oxygen mask fast enough.

Another test involved the rudder throw and aileron roll (stop watch). Later, the automatic approach and landing system would be tested, whether the airline was approved for that or not; the airplane was certified for it. I liked that particularly since one pilot had to guard the controls to take over if it was not responding correctly. The truth was that a pilot could get a flying lesson in crosswind landings with it engaged. I enjoyed lightly holding the controls watching the annunciations in the cockpit change and the aircraft respond accordingly from approaching in a crab to smoothly translating to a side-slip and the pitch moving forward at just the right time putting it lightly onto the runway with the upwind gear touching first. It was like an old instructor telling you to fly the airplane while he is also flying the airplane and learning from the resistance in the areas where you are trying to do something that is different from his movement.

If all the tests were satisfactory, the next test would be by an acceptance pilot sent by the respective airline. If he accepted the airplane, it would never enter the Douglas production facility again for any reason, including that flight.

It was to be the only flight test I would be part of. I was being assigned to fly for Garuda Indonesian Airlines in Jakarta. I learned that the DC-10 pilots who did not have to fly consecutive trips were living in Singapore, while most of the DC-9 pilots, who were flying domestic Indonesian and flying consecutive days, lived in Jakarta.

Looking at the hotels when I got there, the choices seemed to be the Hilton with no outside air or decks, the Ming Court where I decided to go, or the Shangri-La which exceeded the allowance that Douglas would pay and the difference would be made up out of pocket.

I chose the Ming Court since it had outside decks for fresh air and sunshine and checked in over there. They had nice accommodations and a funny and friendly doorman. He was costumed in something out of the *Arabian Nights* and had a large gilded sword on his hip, a turbaned headscarf, and a black wooly beard that must have been real.

The first time I left on a trip, I was also costumed, so we both bantered about with me calling him, "Captain Sinbad," and him calling me "Your Excellency." The waiting cab driver took off like a shot after Sinbad said something and closed the door. I expect he told him to go quickly to the airport. I have been on rides like that particularly in Spain when our company representatives wanted us to get all of our legal crew rested, so as to not have any reason to delay the flight the next day. They would say in Spanish, I would guess, that if we were not delivered in half the time it normally would take that the crew would not tip them or something like that because I have been on more record-breaking, tire-squealing rides to and from airports than I care to think about. I wanted to talk to Sinbad to tell him I had a bad heart or something.

Arriving at the airport, I would walk through the ticket counters and then a door behind them to pick up my first-class ticket to Jakarta, then walk out a back door onto the ramp and board the airplane. On arriving at Jakarta Airport, we would park next to a DC-10 that would be my airplane, and when deplaning, I would walk across the tarmac and put my bags onboard. Then I would walk into operations, past the prayer room, into Dispatch, where we talked aviation English and got my weather folder and flight plan. Going out the same way, I would climb on the airplane and read the *International Herald Tribune* for an hour until my crew showed up. They would arrive in cars that had picked them up at their homes, with the cockpit crew in a car and a bus for the cabin crew. The people did not have or use their cars the way we do.

The first flight I took out, I did not see the flight engineer make a walk-around of the aircraft, so I asked him how his walk around was and he said that the paperwork showed no problems. I said, "What paperwork?" He took it out of his briefcase and said that the Ground Engineer signed it off. I said okay, but I was thinking that stinks. I planned to do a walk-around myself in the future instead of reading the newspaper. We were flight planned for Melbourne, Australia, and then back to Sydney where we would layover for two days. All went well, the cockpit spoke aviation English and asked for permission to speak in their native tongue before they would do so. They would always ask, even when I told them it was not necessary. They were very good in a rigid way, nothing deviated, all standard calls and actions and very sensitive to anything I said that could be critical of their performance. They were more than competent in assistance, but I wondered how the chain of command would work without me. There were twelve cabin crew; two of them were men. All of them were very professional. One of the men served the coffee the entire time while the other man would take our meal requests. I would get a special English meal, unless I requested otherwise. A female, however, served the meals, and I noticed my cockpit crew laugh after she left and talk back and forth in whispers for a while. It was almost like school kids talking. Different culture, same interests.

After Melbourne and finally getting into Sydney, we stayed in downtown Sydney almost next to that ball of water fountain that is seen in postcards, etc. I had a large multi-room suite all to myself; I would never see the crew again until it was time for the crew bus to the airport. This was true for the several months that I flew there. I did not mind; I can be a private person, yet I talk easily to strangers so I am never ill at ease. I would go to the opera house, ride the catamaran to the outer island and go to the zoo. Then later I would go to an Aussie bar that I made some friends at and then early to bed.

I got up one night and went into the kitchen, where I hardly ever went, to get some ice and water. In a building next to me, a woman was just coming into her apartment. She closed the door and turned into a room that suddenly lit up with a light I guess she had just turned on. She went to a refrigerator and opened the door at the same time taking off her sweater, blouse, then unbuckled her bra and stood looking into the icebox. She took out a six-pack of beer, put it on a table, and went into another room that I guess was dark or had no window. I went and got my ice water and went back to bed. I thought about the six-pack. She did not go to bed; there was a six-pack getting warm. Just for satisfying my analytical analysis, I had to see if the beer was still out. I got up again and looked. She was standing naked in the living room on the phone. I used all of my willpower and went to bed; I had to fly in the morning.

The flight from Sydney went directly to Denpasser, "Bali," and from there to Jakarta, but too late to get back to Singapore, so I would stay at the Jakarta Hilton until the morning.

I said, "Good morning, Captain Sinbad," "Your Excellency, welcome home," said Sinbad.

Many other flights I made were flown to Bombay, India, and to Hong Kong. I took a vacation and went to Bali; it was very beautiful yet primitive at the same time. When first arriving on a Garuda flight, we were met at the exit from the small terminal. "You need a guide, sir and miss? This is a very fortunate time to come, sir. I show you the most important happening. It starts within the hour, sir." "What is this happening you are talking about?" "It is a cremation, sir, very important day for us, sir." I am thinking that watching haircuts would be more fun, but his excitement had persuaded us to follow. A short taxi ride and we were at a large field. There were decorated models of animals, mostly bulls, and very festive friends, relatives and onlookers. The remains, mostly bones, were placed inside the hollow insides of these animals, and then fires were built around them. Most remains were buried previously, waiting for relatives to accumulate the money to fund these cremations, which, in the smoke, releases their souls to return again. The interesting thing was the joyful singing and happiness of the people.

Bali was beautiful and unspoiled, and as we walked around the trails, you would find many different craftsmen and women. Some were making wooden statues with a Belize look that was different from others in the world. The grass was green and neatly kept, although I did not see any signs of any tools or mowers to care for it; maybe it was just there. No civilized sounds of engines, horns, or really anything. Smiles from passing strangers. A place for the mind as much as the eyes.

Bombay, my gin, and a French-fry layover. I did not go outside. I did not eat in the restaurant. I instead went to the upstairs lounge and ate French fries while sipping gin, no ice. I do not get sick. The day of departure I was down early reading the *International Herald Tribune* when my Pan American friend from Heathrow was leaning over the back of the chair, "George?" I turned to look. "How are you?" "You seem to get around too," I said. Getting up, I turned towards him, as he said, "No elephant?" "No, there is no more elephant. I am now with Garuda Indonesian Airways." "Starting as Captain again, I see," he said with a fake subtle annoyance. "Yes, well it is part of my overall job," I started to say, but a crew member called to him about the bus, and he waved and ran off. I guess he either thought I was with the CIA or that I could not hold a job, or heck, I did not know what to think.

Back in Singapore, I was told that I would have to start flying some of the Sri Lanka, Jeddah Hajj trips, but as it turned out, I did only one of those and came back to running a series of Hong Kong turns. Then back to my favorite Melbourne, Sydney layover. I had started eating frequently at a French restaurant that was a little pricey but very much worth it. I would do the catamaran trip simply for the boat ride, sometimes coming right back. My suite at the hotel was always there by virtue of there always being a Garuda captain there every night, and so it was blocked by contract. If I woke up during the night, I always debated if I should get up and look for the girl across the way.

Back in Singapore, I went over to visit Rod Mims and his family. Rod had been a DC-8 pilot with ONA but one that I had never had the chance to get to know well. Here in Singapore, we had become good friends. Rod had been hired at Douglas before me by virtue of being furloughed first. Hence the rule of always treating the junior pilots by seniority very nice since they might be the boss on the next airline. That was about to play out in the future for me. Charlie Bare, whom I only knew by name because he was flying copilot on the DC-9s long after I was long gone on the DC-8s, was also here in Singapore, but I had only seen him once in person when I first got here.

I was enjoying the flying, but there was something missing. I was a stranger in the cockpit aside from the aviation English and besides all the courtesies I was shown. There was no small talk. I asked them what they did on the layovers. They would get together in one another's rooms, eat ice cream, and play Mahjong—a game of tiles that I learned to play in the Philippines but not while eating ice cream. I noticed that they seemed to be carrying extra luggage on these Sydney trips, and so one day I asked them why. I was told they carried meat back home this way, which was better and much cheaper in Australia.

Sometimes when it was my leg to fly, I would disconnect the Auto Pilot Approach at Glide Slope Intercept. It was easy to do. The button was close to where the flying hand (Left for Pilot & Right for Copilot) would be located and for that very reason. It would be difficult to notice either pilot doing that, but the result would be very noticeable. A low volume siren would go off until the button was pushed again or the paddle switch re-engaged. I would click quickly so they would look at me to see if I did that, and I would say it was okay. "Oh no sir," they would say as they tried to re-engage the paddle switch. We are not allowed to do that until we were at 500 feet or lower. I would tell them that I had to fly a certain number of manual approaches as a Douglas pilot, and that it was all right. They would not interfere further, but I knew they would report that to the Chief Pilot which the Chief pilot liked to hear anyhow, so he could be sure his policies were still in place. Push one button and test three systems.

My 90 days were almost up, and I asked Rod if I could buy something that he could put in his allotment to ship home. He was on a year stay that would be ending shortly also, but Douglas would ship many things home at no expense on that tour of duty. He allowed that it would be all right.

I had one more Hong Kong turn to do and wondered if this might be the last time I would do this famous approach. There was talk of a new airport to be constructed during the next few years. It was effectively an ILS approach into a mountain where there was a huge checkerboard painted. Upon seeing the checkerboard at a certain altitude, you were free to turn toward the airport and visually land. If not, you must execute a detailed missed approach procedure and climb to a specified altitude. We had the checkerboard and slid down the mountain slope at about the same angle that it and the houses and apartments that were built on it, drying the hanging laundry that was strung out on revolving clotheslines with our jet exhaust. It was also best to get down near the approach end de-crabbed and sideslipped as necessary, ready to put it on the runway without hesitation. This would get the passengers to the terminal faster because you would be able to taxi back rather than go through a ditching drill in the bay.

While having coffee in the terminal, killing time to get back on the aircraft for the return to Jakarta, another Garuda captain came along and said, "Mind if I join you?" "Certainly not," I said. He talked a little about the duty free there in Hong Kong, and while he talked, something was wrong with this picture: we only flew up here once a day. I asked him when he got there, and he said, "With you, what do you think?" I said, "Were you deadheading?" and he said, "Captain, I was working your cabin." I said, "You are not a captain?" "No sir." "But you have four stripes." He put his sleeve on the table and said, "I am the purser, and I have four stripes but they are not as wide as yours." I suggested we change jackets and see if any of the crew noticed, but the sizes were too different. He liked that idea, and we laughed about it whenever we met. I would say, "Good morning, Captain," and he would say, "Good day, Purser."

MCDONNELL DOUGLAS
CORPORATION

7 May 1979
C1-255-GRJ-L317

To Whom It May Concern:

Captain George Flavell has been employed by Douglas Aircraft
Company as a DC-10 Captain from 2 August 1978 to 18 April 1979.
During that time he performed the duties of Line Captain with an
African airline flying between London and cities in Africa and with
an Asian airline, operating on routes from Sydney to Bali, Jakarta,
Singapore, Sri Lanka, Bombay and Jeddah. He was required to use
the particular procedures of each airline in turn, and to fly with the
native crews of each country. A portion of this period covered the
annual HAJJ flights to Jeddah where it was necessary to fly long hours
under the handicap of a constantly changing schedule. As such, he was
required to work without supervision and make many critical decisions
based solely on his experience and judgement, which has been consistently
sound.

Captain Flavell worked hard and has been a cooperative and dependable
employee. He is well liked by both the customer crews and his fellow
pilots. We regret his departure.

G. R. Jansen
Director
Flight Operations

162

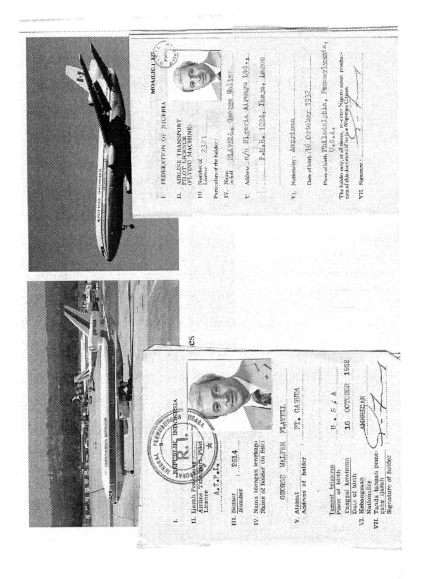

The fact was they were different but not that noticeable; this was not a problem as long as your concern was getting a cup of coffee versus finding someone who could fly the airplane. National Airlines, not to be confused with Overseas National Airways, had a uniform of black stripes on black uniforms. Those crews had problems with that. I had heard a few non-uniformed people say we were trying to look like Mexican Generals. My answer to that was, "If you want to be seen as a pilot, you should look like a pilot; if you want to be the leader of a Mexican army, you better damn well look like a Mexican General." A further example: If I have job as a doorman, I want a uniform that looks like a doorman, not like a well-dressed executive or any other specific form of clothing or uniform.

When I got back to the Beach, I was told my next assignment would likely be Afghanistan flying for the National Airline Ariana. I did not comment, but I had seen enough of that part of the world that I was not going to Afghanistan.

One morning I was asked to accompany one of the old-timers with Douglas to observe the operation of the Flight Simulator. As he instructed the pilots who were in training, he was also instructing me in how to operate the various and multiple switch choices to accomplish this. As he described his little niche in having this skill as far as days off, etc., I felt like I did with Flight Safety. I would enjoy doing it, but I enjoyed flying much more. As we approached a ten o'clock break, he began explaining what we could accomplish that afternoon, and I told him I would not be coming back that afternoon that I was giving my notice during the break. "Oh boy, you have a flying job, right?" I denied that simply because I did not have anything other than the overall job that this was—a great job with great people learning all the skills to be a good pilot as well as being on the leading edge of new aircraft all the time. But I wanted to do actual line flying with an airline that had English-speaking people that I had something in common with. I only had thirteen years left before the mandatory retirement age for pilots.

Just about lunch, I went in to see Roger Conant. He said I was working for him, but I seemed to be on my own, sort of like he said he was not sure whom he worked for. His door was open, but he seemed to be looking at something very studiously. I knocked on the doorjamb, and he looked up, and said, "Come in and have a seat." I did and waited while he worked on a schedule of some kind that required changes. I said, "I can come back," and he said no, to wait. "I will only be a minute." Finally, he sat up straight and, smiling, said, "What's new?" "I am going to resign." Right, he put his head down and adjusted something on the paper, then suddenly sat straight up, "You are serious." "Yes." "Why?" "It is time." "You found a better-paying flying job?" "No." "When do you need to leave?" "No special time if you need me, but I do not want to run a simulator. It wastes the company's time to be teaching me something I will not be here for." "Why don't you wait until you have a job, then quit?" "It is better that I chase what I want full-time." "How soon do you want to leave?" I looked at my watch and said, "Is noon okay?" "That quick?" "Let me get Flip Johnson in here." I knew Flip from Singapore. They got some papers together, and I said some good-byes and went to the elevator. As I got out at the bottom, Charlie Bare was just getting on. He asked quickly how I was doing. I said, "I just quit," and his face went blank as the doors closed.

I went back to Philadelphia to visit my parents, and the next morning I got a call from an old friend and pilot with ONA, Bill Holloway. He wanted me to be Chief Pilot for a newly formed and almost ready to fly private airline for moving oil patch employees back and forth from Houston, Texas, and Libya. What timing, but I thought that wasn't what I wanted actually, but by following it, I might fly it instead of running it. He insisted that I come and see the offices including mine at the new Houston International Airport. Well I got down there; he even paid my airline ticket and expenses for being there, a class operation where aviation was concerned, and we rode the airport trams around the various areas and stopped while he showed me my office in progress. He was going to get back to me, but it started dragging on a little longer than he had indicated, and the news from Libya was not too good. When I would call Bill, he was right upfront with me and said he did not want to call and lose me, but he also did not want to call and lead me on.

One day I happened to call Milt Marshall and chatted with him. He asked what I was doing, and I filled him in. He said he had an interview with "Mark Royes" with Air Jamaica flying DC-8s to London, Frankfurt and Zurich from Kingston and Montego Bay. He said that he was told to bring any other good ONA pilots he knew, and with that, he had a portfolio to bring me. I said okay, and with that decision, I was employed until I would again quit.

I really enjoyed Air Jamaica and the people that worked there. They really tried to run a good airline, and for the most part, they did. Some things were beyond their control because Air Canada exercised some control, and many political problems in the islands made other things difficult. Underneath their serious approach to business, they still had a great sense of humor. I remember being in the initial ground school for the DC-8, an airplane that most of us had thousands of hours on. The Air Canada ground instructor who was a very serious person carried on about a new person in our midst. He was Captain George, former Chief Pilots, Chief Pilot for Air Canada, and who had forgotten more than we would ever know about the DC-8. He happened to be sitting next to me at that moment, and I quietly introduced myself as a Captain George also, except it was my first name. He was delighted and said so. The ground instructor droned on and on about the differences in the various models of the DC-8s and the different engines on them. He got to the –63 DC-8 and asked Captain George if he could enlighten everyone on the major difference between the other engines and the engine on the DC-8-63. Captain George stood up to answer and everyone turned in his direction.

He described the other engines first, giving all the boring details of pushing the start switch, noting that the start valve opened, the oil pressure rising, N1 rotation, N2 rotation 20%, fuel on, light up (accompanied by a little bump sound) EGT rise, start valve closed, and engine stable. He did this with such seriousness that no one even smiled.

He then went on to tell us to keep that first description in mind and you would be able to tell exactly what the difference was. He paused for just a second to take a deep breath while the ground instructor looked on in rapt attention at this icon of expertise. He said, "Here we go. I raise my finger and place it over the start valve of the engine I am about to start, and as I press it down, you will hear..." and here he imitated the screaming hiss that preceded the low whistle that kept increasing in volume and pitch until the engine lit off and promptly went on to high "C" and beyond, before stabilizing. He went too high in a loud replicate that I swear was exactly the noise the engine made, and the ground instructor looked appalled. He said, "That's it, gentlemen, carry on." Of course we could not carry on; we were all laughing so hard particularly the ones who had flown that airplane for years. Captain George and I were bonded for life after that. Air Jamaica only had those JT3D-7 engines on the −62 series DC-8.

Funny and unfunny things happen in flying that stay in memory, and if for no other reason than if it is worth recording one, it is worth recording the other. My friend who had last seen me in Bombay with a new uniform and airline never crossed my path again, much to my disappointment. Because with Air Jamaica, I flew into Heathrow often and with New York Air and Continental Airlines that had the potential of three more uniforms all with four stripes that could have blown him completely away.

Several months after flying to all their scheduled destinations, I was notified that I would be given a line check up to Miami and back. Although I commuted to Miami to drive back and forth to Sarasota, my home, I had never actually flown a plane to Miami from Kingston. My check airman who had recently returned to Air Jamaica and had been put in charge of fuel conservation would administer the check ride. I did the turn up to Miami and reached TOC and engaged the autopilot at that point. Normally check pilots like to see you hand fly it to altitude (in those days). He started his critique about not trimming the aircraft out before engaging the autopilot, that the autopilot could be holding pressure to hold the course, which could have been alleviated, otherwise saving fuel. I learned something. He passed me but lectured about it a little more than needed.

The next morning I was going to get up about 10 a.m. to catch a ride to Miami and go home. The phone rang at 5 a.m. Crew scheduling wanted me to take a DC-8 that was scheduled for a Miami turn (my airplane to Miami), but it had been fueled for a London flight and had to be swapped back to the Miami schedule and would be overweight for landing if I didn't go aloft and dump several thousand pounds of fuel. Air Jamaica had no trucks for de-fueling. I left a note for my check airman friend that perhaps he was dealing with the wrong people if the company was to save fuel.

With this airline, I flew the longest distances regardless of my flying in the Pacific. The DC-8-62 was the longest range DC-8; it had a short fuselage, but the large wings and engines of the –63. We would get flight plans that showed 11:48 ETE (est. time en route) that would go 12:06 ATE and still have legal fuel for alternate. The example is Frankfurt to Montego Bay. We would leave Brest, France, and not have another landfall until Grand Turk Island.

Getting back to base at the time that you bid the trip looked good on paper, as any commuting pilot with any airline will agree. On this particular day, I was scheduled in with two hours to spare to get a DC-9 flight to Miami. Problem was I only had 15 minutes and had really given up until I went into operations and was telling someone I missed my ride home. Someone in dispatch must have heard and said the DC-9 was delayed with a creeping maintenance problem. I got a pass and got over to the airplane, and the crew invited me right into the jumpseat. I sat there quietly while they talked with the mechanics in the E&E compartment below. Finally, everything was finished, and we were on our way. After takeoff, a F/A came up and asked if I would like to sit in First Class. I did not care one way or the other, but it gave the operating crew more space. I went back. About the time I calculated that the engines would soon be pulled back to begin descent, a flight attendant came to me and asked what meal I would like. She did not look like she was kidding. She left to deal with others. I started thinking, this was a DC-9, an aircraft I used to fly, and I sat in that cockpit and noticed that all fuel gauges including the center tank were indicating full. I had been going to ask about that, but they were talking on the interphone to the guys on the ground. Oh geez, this thing could be going anywhere, Montreal, Toronto, who knew. I went to the forward galley and stuck my head inside their curtains and said, "Tell me what your destination is; this is not a joke." They were teasing me, "Where do you want it to be?" "Sarasota, Florida, I guess is out of the question." Oh yes, finally I learned we were going to New York. "Thanks, that's a relief," I said. "What about Sarasota, Florida?" "Just kidding," I said. I did not want to become a legend. I wondered why Operations had told me that …suddenly I knew. Most of the Contract Pilots commuted to New York.

While flying for Air Jamaica, I was seeing the effects of deregulation impacting the airlines. There was an article in *Aviation Week* that highlighted a new airline that was being formed that might be a threat to a major airline. That airline was defined as "New York Air." For myself, I was not excited about flying for a small airline in New York. Beyond that, I did not follow its progress.

One day a couple of months later, my friend Rod Mims called me in Florida and said that this airline was going to take off big-time. He said that Charlie Bare was the Chief Pilot, and he himself was number two and that I would be number three—if I came onboard (the exact reverse order of seniority that we had at ONA). I had just signed a new contract with Air Jamaica, and I felt like I could dig myself a big hole if I acted quickly. Charlie got on the phone to just say hello and review our exit in the elevator at Douglas.

He said that if I changed my mind soon enough, he would be sure to get me on as number three. I told him what I had told Rod and thanked him greatly for the opportunity.

I had a trip to London with a short layover, and the more I thought about it, the more I was in turmoil. This job gave me a seniority number along with the other Air Jamaican crew members, but only as long as they signed a new contract. This might be my only chance of getting a good number with an American company, and it was no less secure than Air Jamaica who could also terminate the contract on thirty days notice with cause. By the time I was laying over in London, I had decided to take the New York offer, not even knowing what it paid. I could not reach anyone; it was a weekend. I left a message on Charlie's phone, and on Rod's phone.

I was home in Florida late Sunday night. I just knew there would be a phone call on Monday morning, and I would have to decide a not-so-easy decision on that phone call alone, with no delay, no hesitation. I was pretty much decided. Now I only would have to deal with a contract that I had signed and could be held to as well as no notice because I sensed the need to be in New York was immediate.

The call came; it was from Charlie, and there would be no pay until the airline got off the ground, but we would be "Founders" and receive stock. The pilots would be in ground school soon, along with us, so we could be re-qualified. There were lots of manuals to write and deadlines to meet. The three of us would train and type rate all the pilots, and as

Air Jamaica DC-8-62

CCA.6

I. **TERRITORY OF ISSUE:**
JAMAICA

II. AIRLINE TRANSPORT PILOT'S
LICENCE (FLYING MACHINES)

III. Number of   116
licence

Particulars of the holder:

IV. Name   FLAVELL, George Walter III
in full

V. Address: 135 North Lane

Osprey, Fla. 33559

U. S. A.

VI. Nationality: U. S. Citizen

Date of birth: 16th October, 1932

Place of birth: Philadelphia Penna. US.A.

The holder may, at all times, re-enter the territory of issue
upon production of this document.

VII. Holder's signature:

we grew, we would check out and get approved additional flight instructors and check airmen. It would not be easy; it would not be fun. It had to be on time. Our first revenue flight was planned for December 1, 1980, and once that started, it was like a steel mill. Once it was started, it could never be stopped without complete disaster.

I called Air Jamaica and talked to the Vice President and told him that I had just renewed my contract, and I would honor that if I had to, but I had just been offered a job as a manager starting a new airline and would like to get out of my contract, unless I was absolutely indispensable. He assured me that I was not indispensable, and he would invalidate the contract. I sent my uniform and other materials back to Kingston, with the exception of my wings, which is part of a number of others collecting dust in a wall frame of many. If I had kept all the hats, uniforms, flight bags, manuals, charts, and memos, I would have opened a museum, which I partly have in the attic.

George Flavell
FOUNDER

Ó NEW YORK AIR

Capt. George W. Flavell
Flight Manager

Telephone 212-565-3574
LaGuardia Airport · Flushing, New York 11371

CHAPTER 11

New Airline Startup

December 18th, 1980 came, and I flew a DC-9 ferry flight to Washington, DC, carrying the President of New York Air, Mr. Neal Meehan, and a pilot cockpit observer, getting legitimate FAA observer time. Also onboard were the cabin crew for the next day's inaugural flight.

The next day, December 19th, 1980, we departed on time at 7:00 a.m. It was the very first revenue flight of NYA to be in the air and the first flight of NYA out of Washington, DC, and the first revenue NYA flight to land at LaGuardia Airport, New York.

Charlie Bare would be the captain of the next revenue flight, which would be the first revenue flight out of LaGuardia Airport, New York departing at 7:30 a.m. and the first NYA revenue flight into Washington, DC.

During the next few months, there would be several "Firsts," and in the next few years, many more again.

One of those firsts would be 100,000 passengers a month.

Before the startup, I had either been in Montreal using Air Canada's DC-9 Simulators to train more and more pilots or at Dulles Airport giving them Type Rating rides with the FAA onboard during the midnight hours when an aircraft was free. We three Flight Managers, qualified to do everything, were now six and could do IOE, Line Checks, Prof Checks and Upgrade Training. While all of this was going on, we were being picketed by the Air Line Pilots Association of the other airlines. They said we were new and inexperienced pilots and carried posters showing aircraft wreckage which I have to assume must be from the so-called experienced airlines, since NYA did not have any accidents at that time and never did during its seven-year existence when it was merged into Continental Airlines.

One of the Continental pilots later told me he had been one of the pickets in front of the LaGuardia Terminal on a bitter cold, snowy day with a sign that stated "NEW YORK AIR was UNFAIR TO ALPA." He said he quit picketing in disgust and flew home to Houston, when a little old lady asked him, "How is it that an airline could be unfair to a Dog Food Company?"

Most other airline pilots probably did not know that the first class of about fourteen were mostly all ex-ONA pilots, and that in subsequent classes many were made up of military pilots from the military colleges that had PIC time in the military DC-9s. Many others in later classes had commuter airline experience as Pilots in Command of multi-engine aircraft that saw NYA as demanding of professionalism but at the same time having a possibly more rapid advancement for qualified flight crews than the Legacy carriers of its day.

With expanding routes, we were in need of even more aircraft, and three DC-9s were purchased from Swiss Air. I was sent over to bring the first one back, and I chose Al Wintermyer, an old ONA friend and pilot. We would have a 10-man life raft, a portable HF radio and a strap down Tracor Omega navigation system, for which we had to attend ground school. We would also have the FAA onboard, a navigation inspector.

Arriving in Zurich, we spent the night and left the next morning, filing a flight plan to Shannon, Ireland, to visit the duty-free shop and to refuel. Then on to the so-called Blue Spruce route where we landed at Keflavik, Iceland, for fuel. The FAA guy, a nice gentleman, had announced that he would show me some tricks with the Omega Navigation System, but I did not tell him yet that he would not be touching it on this next leg. We were airborne and en route now to Goose Bay Labrador. It was really not a difficulty of getting lost it was more one of straying off our assigned path. The southern tip of Greenland is a dead-on fix for 60 degrees north, so it would be hard to be lost in a transport-type jet with radar, but never say never. The DC-9-type aircraft we were in had two independent separate hydraulic systems; two systems failing at the same time is impossible. "I had it happen." Rockwell Jet Commander 1121 School told me there was no possible way to have a total electrical system failure. "I had one shortly out of training."

There were others, but the radar was painting the southern tip of Greenland, and we knew that Greenland was not green, but covered by an icecap at least two miles deep. Goose Bay would be next. The Omega navigation system was working well, and I was not going to experiment with it. It seemed rather primitive after the INS Nav systems. In Goose, we refueled and Al became the captain. He jumped in the left seat and after that we were airborne. I invited the FAA guy to sit in the copilot seat and play with the Omega all he wanted since we had Gander ahead of us and with land-based navigation stations it would be no problem. I got up about an hour later, and the FAA guy was mumbling, "It shouldn't be doing this," speaking of the Omega, and Al was rolling his eyes. We passed Gander and landed at Bangor, Maine, for customs and some fuel, and then proceeded to LaGuardia. Al crewed the next two deliveries.

In 1986, New York Air merged into Continental Airlines. At the discretion of Mr. Frank Lorenzo, a mediator was paid to provide a forum for this process to make it as fair as possible to both sides. This mediator would continue as long as progress was being made in the mediator's opinion. At the point that it ceased, the mediator would become the arbitrator and render a decision on the process to be used. In the end, some of the Continental pilots felt that their representatives had let them down, but nothing could be further from the truth. John Campbell and his group held firm to a "Date of Hire" remedy. I was chairman of the NYA group, only because the pilots had approached me as a former ALPA leader and because the company gave me permission to do it since I was part of management. The NYA group did about as well as could be expected by offering counterarguments giving way to Continental's statements of this or that being unfair to them. We finally settled our position, which was a ratio of one pilot for every six of theirs down to a certain level and then a different ratio beyond. As we were ready to stand on that as our position, the Continental group put forth the unfairness of that position because 300 of their pilots were listed in their group that would not likely return and that our pilots would be getting the benefit of that progression which we were not entitled to. Looking at that argument and wishing to finalize our position, I sensed a solution would be to allow a sort of freeze number for our group but then expressed that as a "Leap Frog," a new term that I am now considered "father of." Suddenly one of my group said that would be all right if the rule was that the jump could be completed only if the one advancing is senior by date of hire to the one being jumped. That un-sponsored thought was incorporated by the mediator, soon-to-be arbitrator, in his final rendering.

The Continental group got very serious at this point, huddled together, and finally made the following statement. "If the policy of 'Leap Frog' as described is ever implemented, we would insist on language that 'Once a pilot implements the Leap Frog option, all jumps started must be completed.' " Looking at the smiling faces on the other side, we realized that we had been had. When the laughing stopped, we continued.

The Continental group agreed that date of hire is always the best yardstick and left it at that. The mediator became the arbitrator after that, and all of us were ready for a result, which would take about two weeks.

Everyone on the NYA side felt that we had done the very best we could, come what may. There would be no complaining, only disappointment if some of our proposals went without comment. When the reading came down, I felt that we had gotten a satisfactory result, and I was pleased. However, the number of people on both sides that were unhappy probably meant that both sides had negotiated successfully.

The Other NYA Committee Members:

Captain Tom Stephens

Captain Bill Borrelli

Captain Frank Shanley

The Flight Managers of New York Air had been offered employment by Captain Bob Lemon of Continental Airlines in much the same capacity that they were in at NYA, along with transportation and moving costs. That being a fair and equitable offer, in my opinion, I may have been the first to accept it.

The end result was that Bruce Blue, former chief pilot of the B-737 fleet at NYA, and myself were early participants in joining the Continental Training Department. Bill Hill introduced himself and welcomed us aboard.

The Boeing 737-300 was a relativity new aircraft for both airlines, and now that we were one, we ended up doing the same kind of training that we had been doing right along.

Continental was in the process of recovering from a prolonged pilot strike, and many of those pilots had yet to be trained on this aircraft. Some who heard that there were NYA pilots in the training department were apprehensive about the quality and integrity of those instructors. I hope that I was instrumental in defeating some of those thoughts because I had only one goal in teaching anything, and that was to see pilots succeed.

When Continental got approval for an "Aircrew Designee Program," I was the first to be approved (by virtue of a random order of who flew first).

After slightly more than two years in Continental's Training Department, there was a cutback in personnel, and I was sent

U.S. Department
of Transportation
Federal Aviation
Administration

Certificate of Designation

Reposing special trust and confidence in the integrity, diligence, and discretion of

GEORGE E. FLAVELL

who has been found to have the necessary knowledge, skill, experience, interest, and impartial judgment to merit special public responsibility, I hereby designate as

AIRCREW PROGRAM DESIGNEE - B-737

with authorization to act in accordance with the regulations and procedures prescribed by the Federal Aviation Administration relating to this designation.

Issued at HOUSTON, TEXAS

Dated 12-18-87
CANCELLED 1-23-89

Certificate No. SW-64-CAL-2

By Direction of the Administrator

WALTER J. PRICE

MANAGER, SW-FSDO-64

back to the line. Each day that I flew the line, the more I realized again that this was what I should be doing anyhow. One morning a few months later, I reported for a trip and found my mail folder gone. I went into the chief pilot's secretary to see what happened, and I was told I was back in the training department. I quickly corrected that situation and flew my trip, for which I had reported.

I was back to the line to stay now, and it only got better. Soon we were flying in Central America, an area that I had not flown in previously. Tegucigalpa, Honduras, was the first city I was checked out on. It is up in the mountains, and although there is an instrument approach for it, you still have to circle in VFR conditions to land. The final approach is made descending the slope of a mountain to the approach end of the runway, and the far end of the runway is a cliff.

Sounded worse than it really was, and the B-737-300 is the perfect aircraft for it. I really enjoyed going in there because it reminded me of the way flying was years ago where you really had to maneuver in some cases to avoid hazards of various sorts (Kansas City Airport and Detroit City Airport).

Before long, we were serving every country in Central America. One of the better routes required a third pilot since it would exceed eight hours flight time, from Houston to Guatemala City to San Salvador to Los Angeles, California. One day on one of these flights, coming back from Los Angeles, an interesting and yet sad event took place. While parked at the gate in Guatemala City, waiting to load passengers, the local (native) gate agent came into the cockpit and asked me if I wanted to put the guns in the seatback (mine). I said, "There are no guns allowed to be carried topside in the aircraft. They must be unloaded, in a locked container, following all of the company's rules and regulations and then put onboard in the belly." He said, "We always do it this way, Captain." Feeling this must be a job for "Superman," I pictured throwing my cape over my shoulder, and I assured him we would not be doing it this way today. I told him to take those guns off the aircraft, to follow the procedures, and to send a supervisor to the cockpit. He said he would. No one ever came out, and I assumed that he talked to the supervisor, and that it was corrected at that level.

Nearing Houston, one of the flight attendants, who usually flew London and European flights, where much paperwork is required for everything, came forward and said, "We do have to clear customs here in Houston, don't we?" I indicated that was correct and asked her why she had doubts about that. She said, "I am wondering how to handle the paperwork where the guns are concerned." "What guns?" I said. "The guns that are in the drawer in the galley where the agent said

179

you told him to put them. Whoa, I could see Superman was in trouble now. I turned to the copilot and asked him to fly and handle the radios while I talked to the company.

The company answered my "In Range" call with a question. "Do you have guns in the cockpit, Captain?" "No there are no guns in the cockpit, but I just found out they were placed in a galley drawer without my knowledge, so you might want to call company security about this for customs coordination." "That will not be necessary, Captain, as we have the FBI, FAA, Airport Security, Company Security and the Houston Airport Police here waiting." "How could you know about this when I did not know?" I asked. "The Guatemala office sent us a landline message confirming that an agent had been given permission to put them in the seatback behind the captain." "Well he must have sent that before he came to the aircraft because I chased him off telling him to take them to his supervisor for proper handling and that, in any event, they are never transported topside." "Well you can handle that once on the ground at gate 14, Houston out."

I called the cabin and had the flight attendant come into the cockpit where I briefed her on what had transpired and suggested that she make an announcement as we approached the gate for everyone to remain seated, regardless of the cabin door being opened because an agent would be boarding the aircraft first to make an announcement.

The sad part was that an innocent couple was arrested and taken off the airplane by federal and local authorities when the happenstances were beyond their control. I heard much later that they had been compensated greatly for their embarrassment.

Just flying the line and enjoying it continued until my coming birthday in October 1992 when by FAA mandate all pilots have to retire at age 60. Continental went far beyond what I would have expected for my last trip. I had my parents on my flight from Tampa to Houston with my son-in-law, Michael. My daughter who is a Continental flight attendant was assigned to this trip to work it.

In Houston, my Chief Pilot, Dennis Turnbough, was there with Linda Meier, who had really run the Chief Pilot's office for years, as well as a number of my pilot friends. There was cake with an airplane and my name on it, non-alcoholic champagne, and a nice model airplane identical to the one I just flew. Just a very pleasant few minutes taken out of their day but they went way out of their way to prepare and be there. There had to be notifications to the traffic control centers because both Jacksonville and Houston centers said goodbye and sent me tapes of our airborne conversations.

CONTINENTAL AIRLINES FLIGHT 1593
October 15, 1992

***   SALUTE TO YOUR CAPTAIN   ***

Your flight today is under the command of Captain George Flavell who will be celebrating his 60th birthday on Friday, October 16, 1992. Federal Aviation Regulations mandate an airline pilot's retirement at age 60, therefore, this will be Captain Flavell's last flight as a Captain for Continental Airlines after more than 35 years of dedicated airline service.

Captain Flavell joined the United States Air Force in 1950 and became an "Aviation Machinist." Following the end of the "Korean Conflict" and his honorable discharge from the USAF, Captain Flavell began his airline career as a mechanic for United Airlines and began taking flying lessons. In 1957 he was hired as a First Officer by "Aloha Airlines." Through the course of his career Captain Flavell went on to fly for Allegheny Airlines, Overseas National Airlines, Douglas Aircraft Company, Garuda Airlines, Nigerian Airways, Air Jamaica, New York Air, and Continental Airlines. He has accumulated over 23,000 hours of total flying time and over 21,000 hours as Captain in a variety of aircraft including the Douglas DC-3/DC-8/DC-9/DC-10, Convair 240/340/440, Boeing 737, Lockheed Jet Star, and Israele Aircraft Westwind.

During his career Captain Flavell has flown all over the world and also shared this knowledge and expertise as an Instructor in the Continental Training Department before returning to the line to finish his career doing what he enjoys most - flying.

Please join Captain Flavell's daughter Leslie, your Flight Service Manager today, and the rest of us at Continental Airlines in a salute to your Captain for a career that has been marked with personal achievement as well as dedicated service to our Company and its customers.

Robert R. Ferguson
Vice Chairman and
Chief Executive Officer

Lewis H. Jordan
President and
Chief Operating Officer

Frank J. Lullo
Vice President
Flight Operations

182

The last day, the last flight home,
Tampa, Florida to Houston, Texas.
The first and the last time
Daughter and Father
would work together as
Captain and Flight Service Manager.

CHAPTER 12

A New Flight Engineer

Without ever having been an engineer, I had to study for a written test and then train in the simulator in that position, which Continental offered to me. Finally, there was the practical test, and then I was a Flight Engineer on the Air Bus A-300. I had an excellent instructor, Captain Walter Ellis, in this regard. Plus an excellent aircraft. It was designed not to need a flight engineer. If anybody was ever instinctively endowed with the skills needed to do nothing, and be paid, it is I. I have a recommendation from an old English teacher who, when she was living, was sure that I would have excelled at something like this if I would just show up. She would be so proud. I showed up for the next three years whereupon my pilot retirement would have been affected by averaging my past captain pay with my flight engineer income. So, I felt forced to do nothing again by going into full retirement. (A term my wife is not familiar with.)

I can safely say all of the above because the A-300s were sold at the end of my three years, otherwise there would be a crowd of F/E's with ropes looking for me. The seat did have a fair amount of work. Some of that work was generated by the airlines themselves, some to assist the pilots since the flight engineer was a required position, and some that had been designed by the manufacturer to be pilot actions or automatic, now redesigned prior to certification back to the engineer panel.

It was really a fascinating opportunity for me to fly that position and for getting to know the Continental pilots that flew the Air-Bus that I would have never known. They were a great bunch that reminded me of the ONA pilots when I had been a copilot on the DC-7. Highly qualified and professional, though most would laugh at that description, and I would expect them to, because what they did was make everything look easy and with communication skills that made the cockpit seem more like a family going for a Sunday drive in the country. This scenario could easily change back and forth to technical terms that an ordinary observer would not recognize, and so quickly and smoothly that in one sentence you might hear both.

I still wore four stripes but no eggs on my hat. I would have preferred changing to two stripes if that had been the culture, because that would have designated my position. The reason I say that is that it causes confusion among ground, other flight personnel, and passengers at times of communication. There is no need to dwell on that now because the era for that happening no longer exists. The largest of aircraft now only carry two pilots. I could really make the case for a third pilot with mixed duties of cabin/cockpit but that might already be resolved by the "Multiple Crew" now used on the long flights that are now possible. I feel very lucky to have had the chance to be a Flight Engineer if only for the perspective of watching the pilot crews in a normal flight environment. I say 'normal' since I have done a lot of official observations as a check airman, at different times and with different airlines, and there is no way to know if what is being observed is the norm or a reversion to "flying by the book" for check ride purposes.

The Engineer has two big advantages where he is seated. He opens the door for the flight attendants and eats his meals on a table. The part about opening the door for the flight attendant is handy because you can get your coffee order in even if they are busy up front.

CHAPTER 13

Enjoying the Minor League

Sarasota, Florida, 1999, Dolphin Aviation hired me to work behind their customer reception desk handling aviation fuel orders and payments, transit and permanent aircraft tie-down or hangar space questions, aircraft catering questions or handling many more things that would come up. I had applied for the job to have something to do and to hang around the airport, which did a remarkable amount of transit corporate aircraft refueling and overnight layovers. I was slightly interested in perhaps getting re-qualified as a General Aviation flight instructor, but I was not sure I wanted to work or talk that much.

A few months went by and I noticed that Gene Critelli, a flight school owner, arrived every morning at 8 a.m., stopped to get free coffee from Dolphin, talked to me a little, and went on his way.

The winter months were coming when things would really get busy with the corporate aircraft business, and the young lady that I worked for asked me to get ready to train some new hires on the counter. She was an excellent employee and knew the discounts that various people had in place and whose plane was in what hangar, and she would refuel aircraft herself, if necessary. It was time for me to explain my competence or lack thereof before I could make her look bad. I told her I liked the job. I enjoyed working for her, and she deserved better help so I would be quitting. I think she looked relieved; maybe now she did not have to fire me.

I went over, talked to Gene Critelli of Eagle Aviation, bought some books that I would need to refresh myself with, and scheduled a check ride for the following week.

When we came back from the check ride, he pointed out whatever I needed to practice if there was something I just did not remember, and I took a check ride with Dave Whitman who renewed my CFII and started to work at Eagle Aviation.

I did not want to take work from any of the instructors that were hanging around all day, and I wanted preferably to work with Instrument Students since Eagle had a nice Cessna 172SP with GPS and the necessary equipment to fly real IFR.

I remember getting my instrument rating without ever flying in real instrument conditions and that lacked something. Some instructors have said that they are afraid that it might encourage the student to go into real instrument conditions when they should not. I wondered if they taught their children to swim. From November 2002 to October 2003, I had completed all of the instruction to train and sign off on the following Licenses or Ratings all of which were passed on their first attempt.

3 ea   Instrument Ratings

1 ea   Commercial License

1 ea   Multi-Engine Ratings

1 ea   Certified Flight Instructor

1 ea   Private Pilot License

Gene Critelli, owner of Eagle Aviation in Sarasota, Florida, was one of the finest examples of General Aviation's Leaders. He lived for teaching flying. Fired with enthusiasm and bursting with knowledge and skills, he inspired all that flew with him. Some airline pilots and future airline or corporate pilots will always remember him. His wings are forever folded now, but I am proud to have known him and worked for him.

COMPANY - WHERE - WHEN - POSITION

NEW: RATINGS

(For Aviation Buffs)

USAF – Clark Field P.I. 1951-1953
Aviation Machinist C-47 Depot Overhaul

United Airlines – San Francisco, CA (1954-55)
MACHINIST - DC-7 Engine Overhaul

Fairchild Air Service – Hayward, CA (1955)
New: Student Pilot Lic.
STUDENT PILOT

California Airways – Hayward, CA (1955)
STUDENT PILOT
New: Private Pilot Lic.

California Airways – Hayward, CA (1955-56)
STUDENT
New: Commercial Lic.

California Airways – Hayward, CA (1955-56)
STUDENT
New: Flight Instructor Rating

California Airways – Hayward, CA (1955-56)
FLIGHT INSTRUCTOR

Harper Aviation – San Carlos, CA (1956-57)
FLIGHT INSTRUCTOR
New: Instrument Rating.

Aloha Airlines – Honolulu, Hawaii (1957)
DC-3 CO-PILOT

Allegheny Airlines – Pittsburgh, PA
DC-3 CO-PILOT

Air Dorado – China Basin Sea Plane Base, San Francisco, CA (1958)
New: Sea Plane Rating
FLIGHT INSTRUCTOR, CHARTER PILOT

Harper Aviation – San Carlos, CA (1958-60)
CHIEF FLIGHT INSTRUCTOR
New: Multi-Engine Rating & Airline Transport Rating

Fremont Glider Port – Fremont, CA (1960)
STUDENT
New: Commercial Glider Rating

Golden Gate Airways – San Francisco, CA (1960-62)
VP FLIGHT OPERATIONS
DC-3, Beech D-18s, Piper Apaches

Overseas National Airways – Oakland, California (1962)
DC-7 CO-PILOT

Flight Safety, Inc. – San Francisco, California (1962-63)
FLIGHT, GROUND, & DEHMEL DUPLICATOR
INSTRUCTOR

Kern County Land Company – San Francisco, California (1963-66)
New: Convair Type Rating – FAA Oakland, CA
CONVAIR 240 CAPTAIN
New: L-1329 Type Rating – FAA Oakland, CA
JETSTAR CAPTAIN

JOHNSON & JOHNSON - LINDEN, NJ (1966)
JETSTAR CAPTAIN

New: Douglas DC-3 Type Rating – FAA Allentown, PA
DC-3 CAPTAIN

Overseas National Airways - JFK Airport, Jamaica, NY
(1966-78)
New: IA-Jet 1121 Type Rating – Allentown, PA
IA-JET CAPTAIN – White Plains, NY
New: DC-9 Type Rating – McDonnell Douglas, Long
Beach, CA
DC-9 CAPTAIN – Wright-Patterson AFB, Fairborn, OH
(1967-69)
New: DC-8 Type Rating – United Airlines, Denver, CO
DC-8 CAPTAIN – JFK Int'l Airport, NY (1970-77)
New: DC-10 Type Rating - National Airlines, Miami, FL
DC-10 CAPTAIN – JFK Int'l Airport, NY (1977-78)

McDonnell Douglas Corp – Long Beach, CA (1978-79)
DC-10 CAPTAIN Production Test Pilot
& Customer Line Pilot
(Based: Long Beach, CA)
New: Nigerian Airline Transport Lic. #2321
DC-10 CAPTAIN – Nigerian Airways
(Based: London, England)
New: Indonesian Airline Transport Lic. #2514
DC-10 CAPTAIN Garuda Airways
(Based: Singapore)

Air Jamaica – Kingston, Jamaica (1979-80)
New: Jamaican Airline Transport Lic. # 116
DC-8 CAPTAIN
(Based: Kingston, Jamaica)

New York Air – LaGuardia Airport, NY (1980-86)
Founder & Startup - Flight Instructor, Simulator & Aircraft.
Proficiency Check Airman – Simulator & Aircraft.
Line Check Airman.
DC-9 CAPTAIN
MD-80 CAPTAIN

New: B-737 Type Rating – Dallas, TX
B-737-300 CAPTAIN

(NYA Merged with Continental Airlines in 1986)

Continental Airlines – Houston Int'l Airport, TX (1986-95)
Flight Instructor, Flight Standards, Training.
Flight & Simulator Check Airman, FAA Designee. B737
(1986-88)
CAPTAIN – Boeing 737-300 (Line Pilot)
(Retired age 60, 1992)
New: Flight Engineer – Turbo-Jet Lic.
FLIGHT ENGINEER – Air Bus A-300B
(Retired 1995)

Eagle Aviation / Dolphin Aviation
Sarasota Int'l Airport, FL
(2000-03)
Flight Instructor CFI-I, MEI-I, AGI

This employment was a fitting conclusion to my flying
career. It provided the enjoyment of being in general aviation
again and the satisfying feeling of helping a new generation
of younger pilots to gain necessary skills, and then to help
them find initial employment in commercial aviation. It is
General Aviation where I began in 1955, and it is where I
ended up. The pleasure was all mine. I no longer have to eat
many hamburgers or sleep in hangars; in fact, I no longer
have to show up at all, but I often do for my own reasons. I
love aviation and the people in it.

PASSENGER QUESTIONS

"Did you ever have any close calls?" is one of the favorite questions people ask. I am sure that what they are really asking for are split-second life or death scary decisions that must be made quickly and accurately or that almost kill you. The answer is yes, but not in airline operations.

Most things that happen develop over time, an increasing headwind that increased unbelievably to 250 knots en route to Hilo, Hawaii, from Oakland, California. I had watched it on our INS navigation units and had heard it on HF radio from reports of other aircraft. Eastbound TWA was calling San Francisco Airinc with record ground speeds, and Westbound Pan Am had rejected Honolulu's request to change altitude since he could presumably justify continuing as long as the present conditions stayed the same or better. We were 20 minutes from our ETP when one of my favorite engineers, a Polish guy, was telling me a joke, and before he got to the punch line, he had caught a glimpse of the number three INS on the overhead and quickly swiveled his seat back to his panel. When he turned back, he asked me how much fuel I thought we would have on landing. I told him zero. He said, "You know." I told him what I had been observing over the last 45 minutes. The copilot was now coming into it also. They both said, "What are you going to do?" I suggested that we wait until our flight plan ETP for the record, and to give it a small chance of changing, and then request a reverse course to Oakland, exercising our emergency authority. We did all that and made the necessary calls to company "Flight Following." We had no sooner finished, then a flight attendant knocked and came in with a story about a passenger who had been sipping wine all night and was claiming we had turned around. I suggested that winos do not always get the credit they deserve and told her our situation and not to talk about it for a minute until I talk to the passengers. Later, San Francisco called and relayed a message from AirSea rescue that they would standby if needed, considering it a fuel emergency. I suggested that at our new ground speed, of about 730 knots now Eastbound, we could safely make at least Salt Lake City, maybe Denver, but we were really good for Oakland.

A routine flight from New York to London provided a gradual buildup of tensions when new weather came out showing Western Europe and England going down in fog. Stansted Airport went Zero Zero in fog. Quickly requesting Gatwick, we were vectored in that direction until notified that Gatwick was Zero Zero. We requested Heathrow, the same. We then requested the closest airport with suitable landing minimums. They came back with Luton Airport as having 300 feet overcast and two miles visibility but falling. Wondering if the runway was strong enough, we asked if any airlines operated out of there. Told that Monarch Airlines flying Lockheed 1011s were based there, we got our charts out and checked the ILS and runway length anyhow. Just then, London said everything appeared down but Luton, and it was doubtful for long. Finally, on a radar vector for Luton, the ceiling went down to 200 feet and one-half mile. I briefed the crew that I planned to land regardless of the weather, "Any questions, gentlemen, because our situation can only get worse." "No questions, Captain." We were cleared to land. At 200 feet, we had the runway; we landed; the rollout had patchy fog. A close call, not this time.

After a somewhat serious problem in Malaga, Spain, where we had a total hydraulic fluid loss on takeoff and aborted the takeoff, we had that system line replaced and were back in the air within two hours. The passengers had been wined and snacked and were now en route to Shannon, Ireland, where we would refuel once more to go to Chicago. The flight engineer did a quick post flight and found a fuel leak on the number three engine firewall and suggested changing a fitting, which I agreed with. It would delay us about an hour, but with the Shannon Duty Free, it should be a happy delay. As I left the aircraft to go in the shop myself, I was confronted by a group of people that wanted to talk to me. One man in particular was telling the group and me that this aircraft was unsafe and that he was getting off and going on Pan Am. The fact that it needed repairs every time it landed was proof enough for him. They all started in, and I held up my hands and said, "Okay it is a logical thought, so let me discuss it with you. It is not every time it lands; it is just the last two times." They jeered and I interrupted, "Hear me out. I am on your side; let me speak; the first delay was serious and unavoidable and was fixed. This delay is caused only by me. I could have let my engineer fix it in five minutes or replace the part, and I told him to replace it. I have the greatest respect for this airline because they let pilots make decisions like that. The fact that I treat safety as a higher priority than schedule should give you confidence, and I have your safety as well my crew's safety in mind. Now, let me tell you something very important without interruption please. This is one of the best duty-free shops in the entire world, and you are standing here wasting time because you are all going to get back on the airplane when you hear what I am about to tell you. I am going to get in that airplane and fly it nonstop to Chicago in less than an hour from now. If I make it, and I will. You will have paid for a Pan Am ticket that ONA is not going to reimburse you for. You really do not have to worry about that though because you will all be onboard when that door closes, including the gentleman who says he is going on Pan Am. Now, I get a free bottle of liquor when I allow passengers to deplane and go to the duty-free store, and that is where I am headed now. See you all onboard." "Hey Cap, I'm going with you," was the end of that meeting. They all went shopping.

I love New Yorkers; you never have to worry how you are doing—they will let you know. A flight to Europe was delayed for three hours, waiting for a cockpit crew hastily put together because of uncontrollable circumstances. My crew, all in civilian clothes, was taken by company van right to the aircraft. The flight engineer dropped his bags and began a walk-around of the aircraft; the copilot ran up the stairs and right into the cockpit to get the radio work done and load the flight plan into the computers. I was stopped by the flight attendant in the forward galley who was giving me a list of things they needed to have replenished before we left. Standing there with a blue leisure suit jacket and red, white and blue trousers (1976), I heard a voice from a man in the first row shout, "Are you the captain?" I walked a few steps towards him and smiled, "Yes I am." He said, "Geez, you guys are late for work, and you don't even have uniforms. What kind of crummy airline is this?" He sat there with his stocking feet up on the carpeted bulkhead, holding a drink in one hand and a finger sandwich in the other. I leaned closer to him and said in a stage voice, "Hey, hold it down, will you, this is only a part-time job with me, and I don't want to buy a uniform until I see if I like this kinda work." I winked at the people in the other aisle, and they roared while he sat there with his mouth open, holding his snack and drink. Then I said to him, "Welcome aboard." Charter groups are a different ballgame.

Arriving at Stansted Airport near London, England, I was the second DC-8 of two that were needed to fly this charter group. Our representative came running up the steps saying what a disaster he was having. "All the bags for the people in the first aircraft were put on your flight." I mentioned to him the credit he could take from the people getting off my flight because those bags were already out to be picked up as they entered the terminal. "You're right," and turned, telling people, "Your bags are inside already for you, so quickly get your bags and take them to the busses waiting for you." Pleasing 50% of the people sometimes is a passing grade.

END

195

APPENDIX

ATA	Air Transport Association, Inc
ATC	Air Traffic Control
ATE	Actual Time Enroute
AFB	Air Force Base
ALPA	Air Line Pilot Association (Union)
A&P	Airframe & Power plant License
APU	Auxiliary Power Unit (Electric & Air)
CAA	Civil Aeronautics Administration (Old)
CAM	Civil Air Movement (Military Charter)
CFI	Certified Flight Instructor
CFII	Certified Flight & Instrument Instructor
DOD	Department of Defense
DOPPLER	An Outdated Navigation System
E&E	Electrical & Electronic Compartment
ETE	Estimated Time Enroute
ETP	Equal Time Point
F/A	Flight Attendant
FAA	Federal Aviation Administration (Current)
FDR	Flight Data Recorder (Accident Tool)
FSDO	Flight Safety District Office (FAA)
ICAO	International Civil Aviation Organization
IFR	Instrument Flight Rules
ILS	Instrument Landing System
INS	Inertial Navigation System
MAC	Military Airlift Command (Current)
MATS	Military Air Transportation System (Old)
MEL	Minimum Equipment List
NAS	Naval Air Station
NDB	Non Directional Radio Beacon
RMI	Remote Magnetic Indicator (Compass)
RVR	Runway Visual Range
TOC	Top of Climb (Altitude)
TVL	Lake Tahoe (Three letter ID)
VFR	Visual Flight Rules
VOR	Visual Omni Range (Navigation)